nurtu

(spiritual) wellness

SOUL CARE

Amber Albee Swenson

Published by Straight Talk Books
P.O. Box 301, Milwaukee, WI 53201
800.661.3311 · timeofgrace.org

Printed in the United States of America
ISBN: 978-1-949488-75-3

Contents

CHAPTER 1

Self-Care Vs. Soul Care

The internet, workplaces, and even our friends love to tell us all about self-care.

Breathe. Go outside. Plant something. Listen to a podcast.

Workplaces like mine put simple self-care reminders in our mailboxes. One encouraged: "Drink some water, do a short mindfulness breathing exercise, write down three nice things about yourself. Step outside for some fresh air. Find a video of cute animals online. Listen to a song that makes you smile."

Self-care "is everything you do to tend to your physical and emotional health in the ways you are best able to do so."[1]

That last phrase is the caveat, and it's what makes the

---

[1] Stacey Colino, "Why Decluttering Is Important for Self-Care (and When It Isn't)," Everyday Health (March 9, 2022), https://www.everydayhealth.com/healthy-living/why-decluttering-is-important-for-self-care-and-when-it-isnt/.

self-help world incredibly confusing. After going through dozens of lists, I found oxymorons at every turn.

- Indulge! (Mindfully in moderation)
- Relax. Be lazy. Get up and exercise.
- Zone out, scroll mindlessly, limit your screen time.
- Fuel your body. Make your favorite comfort food.
- Celebrate! Be OK saying, "No, I want to be alone."
- Declutter: clutter leads to higher cortisol levels and more stress, but if decluttering stresses you out, don't worry about it.
- Get your finances under control, but splurge on a massage, buy a cookie from the bakery, treat yourself to a candle from the boutique and anything that makes you happy.

The world is always trying to point us to the path of happiness. Our wants, dreams, and desires are of utmost importance and priority. Why then do we need so many lists? Why are we still unfulfilled, looking for more?

Self-care, even by the definition above, misses an important aspect if it is solely focused on this life and our wants and whims. It neglects the soul and spiritual wellness. If only for this life, at best it offers a periphery suggestion to be mindful, to meditate, and to practice gratitude.

But how can you find lasting peace and joy and rest apart from God?

I don't want to downplay taking care of yourself. So please don't misunderstand me, because God definitely wants us to take care of our bodies. He wants us to eat well and get rest so we are energized for the day ahead. He wants us to have ways to cope with our anxiety or deal with our frustration or anger. He wants us to be aware of caring for ourselves so that we can care and serve others. That is so important. Because how can you do the kingdom work God has for you if you aren't taking care of yourself? And how can you focus on your faith, family, or relationships if you aren't doing some sort of self-care to nurture your mind and body?

But in this book, when I speak about self-care, I'm talking about the kind of self-care that is so focused on self and happiness now that it keeps you from prioritizing your faith. Please think of self-care in that lens as you read this book. Self-care God's way is necessary and good. Self-care the world's way is not. And the best kind of self-care is soul care.

Soul care prioritizes your relationship with God. Self-care (the "I deserve this" kind) embraces indulging and focusing exclusively on you. Caring for your soul requires you to submit to God's will and ways. Self-care focuses on making this life the best that's possible and preserving it at all costs. Soul care reminds you this world is not your home and encourages you to live as a citizen of heaven because your body will die and decay but your soul is eternal.

I want to refer to a section from the gospel of Mark, but first I want to tell you about the man who authored the book (also known as John Mark).

John Mark's ministry start was a failure. We're told he deserted the apostle Paul and Barnabas on their missionary journey (Acts 15:36-41). Sometime later Barnabas wanted to give him another shot, but Paul wasn't having it. It caused such a rift that Paul and Barnabas went separate ways. Barnabas took Mark, and Paul did mission work with a man named Silas.

Later Mark joined forces with the apostle Peter, who referred to Mark as his son (1 Peter 5:13). It's commonly recognized that Mark's gospel is an account of Peter's time with Jesus. At some point, the apostle Paul came around too. In Colossians 4:10; 2 Timothy 4:11; and again in Philemon 23,24, Paul mentions Mark as a useful ministry partner.

So what does Mark have to do with self-care? Well, self-care and the lingo to describe and promote it has morphed into a worldview. Let me give you an example. From a self-care standpoint, a synopsis of John Mark's life might read like this:

After deciding that mission life with Paul and Barnabas was unfulfilling, John Mark stepped away to reinvent himself. Even after major self-improvement, Paul refused to acknowledge Mark. So Mark accompanied Barnabas, who validated his worth. Mark eventually teamed up with the apostle Peter, who gave Mark a voice. Eventually, when Paul evolved from his toxicity, he and Mark reconciled, albeit within the parameters Mark determined.

Front and center in self-care ideology is self. A Christian worldview puts Christ at the center, and God's Word is preeminent. Here are some of the fundamentals of a Christian worldview that stand in stark contrast to the self-care worldview.

Front and center in self-care ideology is self.

Before a holy (sinless, without fault) God, we are all toxic. The Bible says all our righteousness (that is, the best we can do) is like filth before God (Isaiah 64:6). We're all in the same sinful boat, desperately in need of a Savior, which God graciously provided.

In God's kingdom, the greatest are those who serve and deny self. Jesus said, **"You know that the rulers of the Gentiles lord it over them, and their high officials exercise authority over them. Not so with you. Instead, whoever wants to become great among you must be your servant, and whoever wants to be first must be your slave—just as the Son of Man did not come to be served, but to serve, and to give his life as a ransom for many"** (Matthew 20:25-30).

Jesus could have had a very different life. If he was all about living his best life, he would have lived in luxury and made sure to surround himself with people who did what he wanted (Judas wouldn't have made the cut). It wouldn't have been on Jesus' radar or in his best interest to submit to dying the gruesome death he died.

But Jesus wasn't focused on self. He left heaven to come to earth for our sake. He kept the law we couldn't keep to be the ransom for our sin. He died in our place in order that we might be with him eternally in heaven. Nothing about Jesus' life or ministry was self-centered.

In the Christian church, "me" and "my work" is a nonissue. The apostle Paul said, **"I planted the seed, Apollos watered it, but God has been making it grow. So neither the one who plants nor the one who waters is anything, but only God, who makes things grow. The one who plants and the one who waters have one purpose, and they will each be rewarded according to their own labor"** (1 Corinthians 3:6-8).

His point: there aren't any superstars in God's kingdom. Don't consider who did what, because ultimately any success from our kingdom efforts is the work of God.

Jesus served. We serve. We're all doing our part. It isn't more prestigious to be the pastor or to be the missionary or, in my case, the podcaster. The pastor depends on the secretary, and the secretary depends on the worship leaders and the people who run the committees to communicate information. I depend on an editor, a reviewer, and a producer. We are a body with many members, and we are all serving each other and Christ. None of us is more important than anyone else. It's not about us.

Humility then and not pride is the mark of a child of God. C. S. Lewis said in his book *Mere Christianity*, "Humility is not thinking less of yourself, but thinking of yourself less." Paul put it this way: **"Do nothing out of selfish ambition or vain conceit. Rather, in humility value others above yourselves, not looking to your own interests but each of you to the interests of others"** (Philippians 2:3,4).

Nothing. Not one thing. Remove self. Consider others' perspectives and needs. This, my friends, is in stark contrast to the self-care message.

Mark wrote this: **"That day when evening came, [Jesus] said to his disciples, 'Let us go over to the other side.' Leaving the crowd behind, they took him along, just as he was, in the boat"** (Mark 4:35,36).

Right now, you may be saying, "Hold up. How was Jesus considering the needs of the crowd?"

When Jesus left, it wasn't about chillaxing or carving out me time. Just a few chapters before this, Mark reported that the whole town came to Simon Peter's door to listen to Jesus. Many were healed. And very early the next morning, Jesus slipped away to pray. When his disciples found him, he told them they needed to move on because others needed to hear his message.

Another time, the apostle John reported that after Jesus miraculously fed the people, they wanted to seize Jesus by force and make him their king (John 6:15). They wanted a provider king to keep them physically fed, not a spiritual King who would free them from the devil, the world, and their sinful flesh. Because of this, he left the people.

If we were to keep reading this account in Mark, we'd

realize Jesus was headed across the lake to drive the demons out of a man who would become his missionary to
that gentile area. His leaving showed he was in tune to
the Father's will. In another place in Scripture, Jesus took
a route most Jews would avoid in order to meet a woman
at a well who would bring a whole town to Jesus (John 4).

So this was not about leaving the crowd as much as it
was about Jesus following his Father's orders. With that
understanding, let's go back to the account in Mark:

**There were also other boats with him. A furious
squall came up, and the waves broke over the
boat, so that it was nearly swamped. Jesus was
in the stern, sleeping on a cushion. The disciples
woke him and said to him, "Teacher, don't you
care if we drown?"**

**He got up, rebuked the wind and said to the
waves, "Quiet! Be still!" Then the wind died
down and it was completely calm.**

**He said to his disciples, "Why are you so afraid?
Do you still have no faith?"**

**They were terrified and asked each other, "Who
is this? Even the wind and the waves obey him!"**
(Mark 4:36–41)

The disciples' question—"Who is this?"—is the question we'll need to answer too. It will determine how, or if, we'll embrace a Christian worldview that lets the Bible shape our thinking.

Is the God of the Bible a Sovereign God, above all things in heaven and on earth (Genesis 1; Psalm 24:1; Isaiah 55:8,9)? Is he the author of the Bible (John 1; 2 Timothy 3:16,17)? Is he intimately involved in the lives of those who love him (Deuteronomy 31:6-8; Isaiah 49:16; Romans 8:28)? Or is he like Baal, whose prophets danced and yelled and cut themselves in an effort to get his attention, to no avail (1 Kings 18:26-29)?

Was Jesus the perfect Son of God as the gospels record? Did his death mean anything, or was he just another prophet who met an untimely death?

If we believe the Genesis account—that the world was created by God and that shortly after their creation, Adam and Eve plunged the world into sin—and if we believe what God said to Adam and Eve—that he would take care of it so they didn't have to live in sin for eternity—then we are led to God's Word for answers.

What did sin do to the souls of men? What did God do about it? Where is God now?

The Old Testament is the account of God being intimately involved in his people's lives. It contains promises of a solution to sin and prophecies foreshadowing how God would fulfill those promises. Those prophecies offered signs to people so they would know the coming Messiah when he came. The New Testament contains the four gospels, giving an account of Jesus' life, death, and resurrection—proof that he was the Messiah. The New Testament letters further explain God's plan for salvation (the way we get to heaven) and God's relationship with us.

A Christian worldview requires us to hold worldly philosophies up to the Bible to see if they are in line with God's Word. Does this make you uncomfortable? Do you cringe at some of the things in the Bible and ask, "God, do you really expect me to believe that?" Are you struggling to let God be God and rule in your heart?

The world tells us to be self-absorbed and motivated by our needs, wants, and pleasures. God's rule in our hearts is quieting our sinful nature and not going the way of the world but letting God be the first and final authority. God's first command is easy enough to understand. You shall have no other gods. In simple language: God first.

And here's the thing. God's ways aren't difficult. They aren't restrictive or chauvinistic. Jesus said, **"Come to me, all you who are weary and burdened, and I will give you rest. Take my yoke upon you and learn from me, for I am gentle and humble in heart, and you will find rest for your souls. For my yoke is easy and my burden is light"** (Matthew 11:28-30).

God's way offers us rest. If you've ever been caught doing something you weren't supposed to do, you understand the energy guilt consumes. There is a fine to pay or a mess to fix or relationships to rebuild. Going our own way isn't as restful as we sometimes think. But going the speed limit is. And walking away from the gossip so you don't get in the middle of nonsense and drama is. And living with integrity so you don't have neighbors knocking on your door asking you to explain yourself is too.

God invites us to yoke ourselves to him and learn from him. We aren't so familiar with yokes. They are the wooden frame that holds two oxen together. The yoke keeps the two in step so that one isn't way ahead while the other is way behind.

The King of kings invites us to walk beside him, not 100 feet behind his bodyguards or within camera range. "Take my yoke upon you" in today's language is this: "Hey, come here. Right here by me."

Unlike a superstar or world leader or sports enigma who has status that makes him or her unavailable to 99% of us, Jesus calls each of us by name. He walks at our pace. He's all-powerful, all-knowing, all-loving, and he wants to walk with me. And you.

His invitation: "Learn from me."

Do you want to hold hands with the King of kings? Or do you want to try to fill up by watching cute animal videos? It doesn't seem like much of a choice, does it?

FOR FURTHER REFLECTION

1. What in this chapter challenges your way of life or the way you see God? Consider going back through the chapter and underlining or circling anything that does.

2. What drives you? Are you motivated by comfort, fear, security, wealth, God's will for your life, or a combination?

3. All of us, even lifelong Christians, still have learning to do when it comes to Christian living. Jesus embodied humility. In which areas of your life do you struggle to let others have a say? Let me give you two examples. 1) One day I asked a godly, reads-her-Bible-daily woman at a nursing home to leave her regular table in the dining room to sit with a woman who was all alone. She vehemently refused. Even after another woman at her table volunteered to go along, she insisted she stay in her same place and, in fact, convinced the other woman to do the same. Her security in routine wouldn't allow her to see or act in love toward a fellow believer. 2) I love when my children clean the house, just as long as they don't touch my stuff. My piles are a nuisance, but I'm not always open to the prodding from my husband or children to deal with them. Are you open to learning in humility from Jesus as you walk with him? Are you ready to put selfish ambition behind you and consider others more than yourself?

CHAPTER 2

First Things First (a.k.a. Our Problem With Priorities)

The self-care world will tell you to make a comeback. Rise up from the things that have put you down. Make new choices and get yourself unstuck. Never look back.

To a certain degree, the message is good. Every day *is* a new day. What a gift! The prophet Jeremiah told us as much in Lamentations 3:22,23: **"Because of the Lord's great love we are not consumed, for his compassions never fail. They are new every morning; great is your faithfulness."**

No matter how horrible our attitude was the day before, we get to start again each day, and God gives us new compassion every day.

We *can*, thank God, make different choices and be different people too. If you quit eating junk food and work out, your body will change. If you make your appearance a priority, learn about makeup, spend time and money on your hair, and buy trendy clothes, you will probably turn some heads.

The question becomes: What do you want? What are you willing to work at, learn, read, create so you can move forward into a different tomorrow? What would you change?

Seek first the kingdom of God.

The same is true for our soul care—which is so much more important. Jesus said, **"Seek first the kingdom of God and his righteousness, and all these things will be given to you as well"** (Matthew 6:33 EHV). "All these things" is referring to what we will eat and what we will wear and all the things we worry about each day.

Jesus said first seek the kingdom of God. Seek God's rule and reign in your heart. Seek his righteousness. Do things his way.

Luke, the doctor who wrote the gospel that bears his name, investigated the details of Jesus' life by interviewing Jesus' friends and associates. Of all the things he investigated and all the information he deemed important, he included five verses that characterize two women. They offer simple but profound wisdom about worry, stress, rest, and missing Jesus even when he's right next to you. He reports:

As Jesus and his disciples were on their way, he came to a village where a woman named Martha

opened her home to him. She had a sister called Mary, who sat at the Lord's feet listening to what he said. But Martha was distracted by all the preparations that had to be made. She came to him and asked, "Lord, don't you care that my sister has left me to do the work by myself? Tell her to help me!"

"Martha, Martha," the Lord answered, "you are worried and upset about many things, but few things are needed—or indeed only one. Mary has chosen what is better, and it will not be taken away from her." (Luke 10:38-42)

Poor Martha was captured and recorded for all time as a frazzled, stressed-out host. Even so, I love her because anyone on a mission with noble plans, too much to do, and limited time to do it knows the frustration of being paired with a less-than-energetic teammate. She opened her home, not only to Jesus but to his disciples. Her intentions were extraordinary.

But here's an important detail to consider. Martha didn't have an overcommitment issue. Martha had a priority issue. Her service came at the *expense* of time with Jesus. She wasn't thinking about her soul care. She misinterpreted what Jesus wanted from her. Far more than a meal, Jesus wanted Martha's heart. Jesus desired Martha's time.

It's a super-easy trap to fall into. We have good intentions. We think we'll have time. But day after day passes, and we've failed to open the Bible, failed to go to God in prayer.

It's easy for our priorities to get out of whack, not just with the big things but the little, everyday choices too. How many moms spend every waking hour cleaning and decorating the house, making an amazing meal and theme cake for their child's birthday party, only to spend the entire birthday cleaning, cooking, and stressing, and not enjoying their child or the birthday at all? How much time do we put in cleaning and decorating the house, planning meals and holiday schedules, only to forget to thank God on Thanksgiving or to prepare our hearts for Jesus before Christmas?

I have a hard time not getting carried away. It's easy for me to dive all in to a yard project or a role at church or, more recently, my work. It takes something akin to a meteor crashing into my house for it to dawn on me that things are out of whack. I've forgotten about my soul care.

For 13 months I've been working pretty close to full time and sometimes more than full time at a nursing home. On my day off, it's common to get a text asking me to come in. I've been slow to recognize that my work's staffing issues do not mean I need to give up an evening with my family. Work would carry on if I were to drop over dead. My family would not adjust as quickly.

Finally, realizing I was stretched too thin and there

was no way I could continue to work that amount and do the ministry I wanted to do, I sent a text to the scheduler at the nursing home saying I needed three weeks off to work on ministry.

No doubt it was not what she wanted to hear.

When I told my husband and children, there were smiles, "Seriously, you'll be home for three weeks?!"—complete confirmation that of course I needed to spend more time on ministry and family.

How had I gotten this so wrong? We were all elated when I first started back to work a year prior. But back then we were operating under the impression that it would be very temporary. Maybe through Christmas, then March, doubtful it would continue through the summer. Here we were at another Christmas, and my family was wanting their wife and mother and validating that ministry deserved my attention and focus.

Jesus was sitting in Martha's house, but she missed his teaching. She didn't get to hear the ways he was working or his explanation of God's plan for salvation.

We too can busy ourselves with so many good things—cleaning, cooking, working, weeding, planning, and serving—*at the expense* of the more important things, or even the most important thing: time with Jesus. He could walk the streets and do miracles and maybe even step inside our church or school doors, but we'd be in the kitchen or the gymnasium or the classroom or running the snack bar.

Jesus' words are meant to shake us from our distractions. Quit doing whatever it is that you are doing, Martha, Amber, and (insert your name here), if it keeps you from a relationship with Jesus. Jesus doesn't need your soup or your clean house or your seasonal decorations. Jesus doesn't need another deal, another book, or another road trip to the NFL game to schmooze with important people.

Just sit at Jesus' feet like Mary.

John, one of Jesus' closest friends and one of three who comprised Jesus' inner circle, wrote this:

In the beginning was the Word, and the Word was with God, and the Word was God. He was with God in the beginning. The Word became flesh and made his dwelling among us. We have seen his glory, the glory of the one and only Son, who came from the Father, full of grace and truth." (John 1:1,2,14)

That can seem cyclical and confusing, but John's point is this: Jesus is the Word. Every time you open the Bible or listen to the Bible or read your favorite Bible app, you are hearing Jesus, the Word, speak. When you and I fill our days but don't take time to listen to or read the Word, we can read Luke 10:41,42 and insert our names instead of Martha. "'_____, _____,' the Lord answered, 'you are worried and upset about many things, but few things are needed—or indeed only one.'"

Everything else will fall short. We can have clean houses and immaculate yards; we can volunteer more than anyone else and sacrifice and labor for great things, but if we do it at the expense of a relationship with God, we will be woefully disappointed.

Jesus said:

"Not everyone who says to me, 'Lord, Lord,' will enter the kingdom of heaven, but only the one who does the will of my Father who is in heaven. Many will say to me on that day, 'Lord, Lord, did we not prophesy in your name and in your name drive out demons and in your name perform many miracles?' Then I will tell them plainly, 'I never knew you. Away from me, you evildoers!'" (Matthew 7:21-23)

Oh, how busy these people were as they did the work of God! They were prophesying, driving out demons, and performing miracles. These were church people running programs and planning activities. They were at church or in a Christian school but missed the reason for being there. They never got around to a relationship with Jesus. Bible study sounded stuffy. Fellowship activities were where it was at. They learned enough Bible when they were young to get by. They might be on the school board or the board of trustees or serving in the kitchen. They were doers.

The People's Bible commentary on Matthew explains, "It is significant that those whom Christ rejects in the judgment call attention to their own works and expect to be received into heaven on that basis."[2]

We need to be wise with our time. One of Satan's key tactics to keep us from important kingdom work is to keep us busy with seemingly good things. He'll distract us from what is important by making other things more important than they should be.

Jesus continued:

> "Therefore, everyone who hears these words of mine and puts them into practice is like a wise man who built his house on the rock. The rain came down, the streams rose, and the winds blew and beat against that house; yet it did not fall, because it had its foundation on the rock. But everyone who hears these words of mine and does not put them into practice is like a foolish man who built his house on sand. The rain came down, the streams rose, and the winds blew and beat against that house, and it fell with a great crash." (Matthew 7:24-27)

Take note of the distinction: hear and put into practice vs. here but not hearing and, therefore, not know-

---

[2] G. J. and M. J. Albrecht, *Matthew*, The People's Bible Series (Milwaukee: Northwestern Publishing House, 1984), 114.

ing what the Word of God says.

I'll give you a second to let that sink in. Hear and put into practice vs. here but not hearing.

The apostle Paul explained, **"Faith comes from hearing the message, and the message is heard through the word about Christ"** (Romans 10:17).

Faith in Jesus is the means of salvation. It grows as you read and listen to the Word. To ignore the Word, refuse to listen to it, or become too distracted to make it a priority is to build your house on sand. It is to hope you have saving faith on the day you die but not to make it priority. It's neglecting your soul care.

Most of us begin planning for retirement in some capacity when we are still young. We put aside a little each paycheck in order to slowly build enough money to live on when we're no longer working.

And yet we put so little time into our eternal future, even though we have no guarantee of long lives on earth.

If that seems backward, it's because it is. Our first and greatest need is a relationship with Jesus. Nothing is even a close second in terms of priorities. Jesus said that one thing is needed. Mary understood that Jesus in the house was reason to pause, sit at his feet, and listen.

Until we learn to do the same, we'll find ourselves chasing so many unnecessary things.

"What good will it be for someone to gain the whole world, yet forfeit their soul?" Jesus asked (Matthew 16:26).

Soul Care: Nurturing Your Spiritual Wellness

Simply put: earthly achievement at the expense of heavenly glory is too high of a cost.

If you exercise every day but don't read the Bible, your priorities are off. If you go to work, clean your house, scroll through your phone but don't work on your relationship with Jesus, your priorities are misplaced.

This is way easier to remedy than you might think. Set aside 15 minutes in the morning, evening, or any time in between. Morning might be the best option so it doesn't get pushed off the to-do list. But if you get up at 4 A.M. to go to work like I do or if you usually wake up when little feet pitter-patter into your room, evening may be the better option. Read the Bible on your lunch break if it works for you or when your kids go down for a nap. And don't get hooked on 15 minutes. Take what you can. It may be 10 minutes; it may be 30 or 60. That's not the point. The point is getting started.

Pray for God to be with you, to help you, and to send his Spirit to guide you. Then open the Bible and read, slowly, meditating on the words. I stop to look up definitions to make sure I'm getting the whole picture. I'm currently reading 1 Peter. Today I started chapter 2: **"Therefore, rid yourselves of all malice and all deceit, hypocrisy, envy, and slander of every kind"** (verse 1).

I paused to look up definitions for *malice, deceit, hypocrisy, envy,* and *slander.*

Go ahead. Google these words, or if you own a dictionary, pull it out and put it to use.

Malice— ill-will, badness

Deceit— Intentional misleading or beguiling of another

Hypocrisy— a pretense of having a virtuous character that one does not really possess.

Envy— Sin of jealousy over blessings or achievements of others.

Slander— Derogatory statement to diminish or harm another person intentionally or unintentionally

Then I started the process of self-examination. Who am I envying? (I don't know why I started with that one, but I did.)

Why is it such a problem? When I envy, I am scorning the blessings God has given me to concentrate on what others have or are doing. I'm refusing to acknowledge the gifts he's given me and wasting precious time longing for someone else's gift rather than using what I have to serve the Lord and others.

Then I prayed God would open my eyes to the hypocrisy or deceit that may have crept into my heart. What falsehood am I treasuring rather than confronting? Where are my beliefs colliding with my faith walk? What have I brushed aside thinking I'm good enough or that I don't want to deal with that right now? (Tone of voice. I need to work on that. Too often I'm in a hurry and don't talk to my family in a kind tone.)

Have I slandered? I knew right away that I had. "God, help me to do better. Forgive me for so easily falling. Tame my tongue and put a guard over my lips so my mouth better serves you."

Concentrating on just this one verse will open your heart to the mind of God. Malice, deceit, hypocrisy, envy, and slander are so easy to fall into, or even embrace, and they will put a wedge between you and God. Remember how he invites us to walk with him and learn from him?

Peter gives us guidance to do that in the next verses. **"Like newborn babies, crave pure spiritual milk, so that by it you may grow up in your salvation, now that you have tasted that the Lord is good"** (1 Peter 2:2,3).

The note in my study Bible was helpful here: "*Crave*. The unrestrained hunger of a healthy baby provides an example of the kind of eager desire for spiritual food that ought to mark the believer. *spiritual milk*. Probably referring to God's word (1:23,25). The author is speaking figuratively. Milk is not to be understood here as in 1Co 3:2; Heb 5:12–14—in unfavorable contrast to solid food—but as an appropriate nourishment for babies. *grow up*. The Greek for this phrase is the standard term for the desirable growth of children."[3]

---

[3] *Concordia Self-Study Bible*, New International Version (St. Louis: Concordia, 1986), 1908.

The emphasis in this verse is to crave spiritual milk so we can grow up.

There isn't much that we should crave like "the unrestrained hunger of a growing infant." Most of what we crave needs limitations. I may crave chocolate, but that doesn't mean I should eat it every time I think of it. Shortly after I wake up, I might think of that series I've been watching (one episode at a time) with my family, but that doesn't mean I should spend the day binging instead of being productive with my time.

Time with the Lord is different. Peter knew how easy it would be for us to be distracted. He knew as well as anyone that if concern for our souls became less and a physical kingdom and its priorities became more, we'd be sidetracked and focused on all the wrong things. So he told us to crave pure spiritual milk, that is, the pure Word of God.

I love listening to Christian music. I also listen to a variety of Christian podcasts and programs. But they are not pure spiritual milk. They are delicious coffee, and sometimes iced tea or lemonade. They add flavor. They lift me up and sweeten the journey, but they can't replace time in the Word.

Praying is our chance to talk to God. Reading the Bible is giving him a chance to speak to us. If we're going to learn from him, we have to let him have the microphone.

God has given us his Word. In his Word we learn his ways. We see how God acts, and we even have access to

God's thoughts. Five hundred years ago, the Bible was inaccessible to most people. Today you can purchase a cheap copy for under $10. A study Bible costs less than dinner and a movie for two. And if you own a phone, you have access to apps that put the Bible at your fingertips.

To prioritize is to designate something as more important than other things. Many of us know God's Word is of utmost importance, but our actions don't align with our beliefs. According to the definition, I think that puts us in hypocrite territory.

Our actions don't align with our beliefs.

Far worse, it may put us on the sand. I love the beach as much as anyone, and if I ever have money and opportunity, you better believe I'd be seriously tempted to buy a house as close to the Gulf of Mexico as I can. But beach houses are only good until the bad storms come. Every year we see the devastation. Wood and stone are no match for hurricanes.

It's one thing to lose a home. It's another thing entirely to forget to feed your soul. If faith comes from hearing the message, then faith withers without the Word. When you stand before the throne of God, "I was going to" doesn't cut it.

Start small or go all in, but start. Take a bite. Before you know it, God-willing, you'll be craving more. And as you get into God's Word, pray that he helps you get all your other priorities in line too.

FOR FURTHER REFLECTION

1. What temptations and distractions keep you from time in the Word?

   Phone

2. What time of day would be best for your time with Jesus?

   Am

3. What other priorities are out of whack, and how can you tangibly take steps to remedy this problem?

   I'm working on making GOD the priority

CHAPTER 3

Worry Gets in the Way of Soul Care

As I was looking through self-care lists, I found advice on focusing on the positive. One list said to watch a funny video or inspirational movie to distract you from other negative thoughts. Another suggestion was to practice positive self-talk by saying things like, "I am enough." One list even said to designate one pen as a magic pen. That pen could only write positive things.

I just don't think any of those things would adequately address my worry. If you listened to my podcast, *Little Things*, from 2020 to 2022, you know I described myself this way: wife, mother, worrier, type A, child of God. When my producer and I created the new opening at the end of 2022, I took worrier out. Worrying is not something to be proud of. It's something to deal with.

When it comes to caring for my soul, worry gets in the way. It keeps me from what I know is true and takes me to the realm of "what if?"

Jesus knew our tendency to worry. That's why he said:

"Do not worry about your life, what you will eat or drink; or about your body, what you will wear. Is not life more than food, and the body more than clothes? Look at the birds of the air; they do not sow or reap or store away in barns, and yet your heavenly Father feeds them. Are you not much more valuable than they? Can any one of you by worrying add a single hour to your life?

"And why do you worry about clothes? See how the flowers of the field grow. They do not labor or spin. Yet I tell you that not even Solomon in all his splendor was dressed like one of these. If that is how God clothes the grass of the field, which is here today and tomorrow is thrown into the fire, will he not much more clothe you—you of little faith? So do not worry, saying, 'What shall we eat?' or 'What shall we drink?' or 'What shall we wear?' For the pagans run after all these things, and your heavenly Father knows that you need them. But seek first his kingdom and his righteousness, and all these things will be given to you as well. Therefore do not worry about tomorrow, for tomorrow will worry about itself. Each day has enough trouble of its own."
(Matthew 6:25-34)

When inflation rises, I can easily think, "Will we have enough money to keep buying groceries?" Rumors of energy shortages cause me to wonder, "How will we get through the winter?" And worry pushes me to work harder, to get more money, because enough might not be enough.

At least when I do laundry, there's a before and after. When I clean the bathroom or weed the front yard, I see change. After worrying, I am in the same situation as before, just more stressed and sleep deprived.

We don't seek God.

In Luke chapter 10, Martha was worried about food. Jesus told her to seek God's kingdom first. Seek God's kingdom like a hot deal on Black Friday. Seek it like pumpkin spice flavoring on September 1. Seek it like patio lights or a fleece blanket or a good haircut.

Problem number one when it comes to worry is that we don't seek God. Or look for him. Or even give him a passing glance.

Jesus said, **"I stand at the door and knock. If anyone hears my voice and opens the door, I will come in and eat with that person, and they with me. To the one who is victorious, I will give the right to sit with me on my throne, just as I was victorious and sat down with my Father on his throne"** (Revelation 3:20,21).

A lot of us hear Jesus knocking and slide to the floor, out of sight, until the knocking stops and he walks away. It happens when we're asked again—sigh—to join a small group at church. Or when the overly enthusiastic older lady catches us on the way to the car and invites us to the women's Bible study. It happens when someone texts you the podcast or the sermon, but you don't have time for that. After all, you are busy working on your worry and gathering the latest news that makes you worry and doing all you can to prepare so the latest rumor won't affect you.

We all tend to think there will be time, someday, when we'll let Jesus in. I witness the distractions (still!) in the nursing home that keep men and women from opening their Bibles. There is bingo and the dice game and whatever shows are on MeTV. There are people in the dining room to talk to and the news and the baseball game and crossword puzzles to keep your mind sharp.

When we don't make time for the Word, we keep Jesus out. And when Jesus loses the top spot, worry quickly slithers in. And worry takes a toll.

How many nights have I seen minutes and hours pass while contemplating scenarios that never play out? Too many. And if it's not sleep, it's energy and time. It's phone calls exploring how horrible things might get. If this happens, this will happen, then that, and most likely that. The world is falling apart, never to recover.

Consider the Israelites in the desert. God miraculously led them through the Red Sea and saved them from Pharaoh's army (Exodus 14). After a three-day hike, they found only bitter water, so God turned it sweet (Exodus 15:25).

When they were hungry, God provided bread from heaven and quail (Exodus 16). He brought water from a rock and gave the Israelites victory over those who were attacking them (Exodus 17). In a short time, God proved himself trustworthy and almighty.

Why would they ever doubt him? Why would they worry about provisions? Why would they wonder if they could take the land he promised to give them? Why would they make another god for themselves when God had been so good to them?

Why do we?

Hasn't God shown himself trustworthy in our lives over and over and over? Hasn't he gotten us through whatever we faced in the past? When we had little, didn't we have enough? When terror seized us (9/11/2001), wasn't he there? Why, then, when looking forward, is it so easy to worry and wonder if he'll provide and sustain? Why do we make gods of news anchors and politicians but fail to turn in faith to the God who holds the world in his hands?

How many times have I seen God work in miraculous, extraordinary ways to keep things from happening? How many times will it take before I KNOW I can trust God?

I worked an evening shift on June 17, 2022. I reported off at 10:30 P.M. and started my hour drive home. Not long into my drive, I remembered my 19-year-old son was at a graduation party with his gearhead friends. I had been at the last graduation party at that venue, and there had been lots of wild driving. With that in mind, I prayed God would protect them all and help those car-loving boys to make good decisions.

At 3 A.M. I woke up and realized my son was not home. I sent him a text, asking where he was. He sent back two pictures: a smashed truck and a bloodied hand.

As we texted back and forth, I found out he was the passenger in a truck that rolled. As I examined the picture, I knew without a doubt that God had graciously answered my prayer. The top of the truck was completely caved in and resting on the seat. My son is 6'5".

If I had known this would happen, no doubt I would have worried. Would he put on a seat belt, or would he get caught up in the excitement and just hop in the truck? What if the seat belt broke and he was thrown from the vehicle or smashed as the truck rolled? What if he was seriously injured and required months of rehabilitation? What if, what if, what if?

Worrying is choosing to forget how many times God has provided, stepped in, and intervened, even when our own foolish actions were taking us down a path of destruction. Even when the worst has happened—when my father-in-law died unexpectedly a few days before Christmas or when I had pneumonia while pregnant with my fourth or when both my parents were diagnosed with cancer ten days apart—God provided and sustained and strengthened.

Worrying is refusing to trust that God is in charge. It

is being consumed by fear about something that might never happen. Think about that. It's choosing to invest in a story that more than likely won't play out, instead of investing in what is happening here and now.

Jesus made it clear that worry is not from God. He's watching and willing to provide. If it's from Satan, I don't want it. And if it's from Satan, it's battling for my soul and a place in my heart and mind that should be fully devoted to God.

James wrote, **"Submit yourselves, then, to God. Resist the devil, and he will flee from you"** (James 4:7). If God is worthy of our trust—and he is—then we can trust him with whatever comes our way. And when

We can trust him whatever comes our way.

things we'd rather not have happen do happen, that's when we can figure out next best steps. Until then, Jesus advises us to live in today.

I've had a chance to talk to several elderly people while working in the nursing home. None of them expected to end up there. As we talk about their lives, they've assured me it's best not to know the future.

If they had known a year prior that they only had a year left to live in their houses, they would have fretted and been sad. Instead, they lived in their homes as long as they could, and when they couldn't, they went to the nursing home. If they knew how long they'd have to live, they'd be worried as the date of their death neared. Better to just live each day and let God take care of the rest.

It might be hard for us planners to realize it, but God knows best. All we really need to know is today. What happens tomorrow will happen. We pray, we trust, and with God's help, we get through—just as he's helped us through everything we've gone through in the past.

Jesus noticed Martha was worried about many things. What would have happened if Martha sat with Mary listening to Jesus? I imagine if Martha sat and listened, there would have been a point when Jesus stopped teaching so Mary and Martha and maybe one or two of the disciples could work together to get a meal ready.

Too often, like Martha, we convince ourselves that everything hangs on us. If we don't do it, the world will stop. How arrogant! I can't be everywhere, and I can't keep the world spinning.

Here's what I can do.

Jesus said he stands and knocks. If we open the door, he will come in and eat with us. I doubt if Jesus and I were eating a meal that he'd be concerned with who won the last election. I know he wouldn't fret over the economy or the direction healthcare is headed. I think he'd tell me to be in the world but not of the world, that my heavenly Father sees me and knows my name. I think he'd tell me my prayers are heard and my Father will do infinitely more than I could ask or imagine. And I think I'd ask about heaven, and he'd tell me that I can't begin to comprehend. He'd tell me to keep going and stay focused, not on myself or on earthly endeavors but on kingdom work and reaching souls. God will bring me home when the time is right.

When we spend time in the Word (soul care!), we do just that. We realign our attitudes with God. We're reminded to love and serve, and we're reminded how much God loves and serves and sustains us. We are reminded that souls are important and to pray for spiritual matters. When we're in the Word, our priorities and our attitudes change, and we aren't so concerned with all the silly things of the world. Worry diminishes as we do what we can with the strength God provides.

And that brings me to an important point. Sometimes our sin causes us to worry about consequences. When those boys were driving crazy and flipped the truck, they jeopardized their lives.

If you are worried about your finances because your spending is out of control, pray God gives you the guidance you need to get out of debt and the strength to overcome your greed. If you're worried about your health because you are overeating or drinking, pray God shows you a better way and gives you the strength to overcome the gluttony. If you struggle with gossip or lying, pray God posts a guard over your lips (Psalm 141:3) and tames your tongue (James 3).

Uncontrolled sin should give us reason for concern, pause, and repentance (turning). The apostle Peter would have had good reason to wonder if God could use him. It took denying his friend and Savior for him to weep bitterly and come to the end of himself. But God wasn't done with him. Far from it! His ministry was just beginning. Peter needed to be emptied of his pride and come to the point of realizing it would be the Spirit in him that would make his ministry effective. He would need to take the back seat and learn to let the Spirit drive.

God is eager to step in when we're ready to change directions. He doesn't wait till we're at our lowest and then laugh in our faces or tell us to come back when we've got it all together. Jesus met with the woman at the well. He touched the leper. He had meals with prostitutes and tax collectors. He appeared to Peter after he rose from the dead. He came back to make sure Thomas, who was struggling to believe, knew for sure.

Worry is an effective tool of Satan to rob us of the peace God provides. **I tell Satan to shut up.** But God equips us to overcome. When worry creeps in, I'm learning to pray about whatever comes to mind and trust God. Then I tell Satan to shut up.

I try not to participate in "what if" conversations. Instead, I remind whomever I'm talking to that God is on the throne and our prayers are heard. If you're bothered, pray. If you see something concerning, pray. If you think someone might be planning something against you, pray God foils the plans of evil.

If you, like me, desire a worry-free life, there's a simple solution. Take care of your soul. Spend time in the

Word to know who God is. Pray. And refuse to give Satan a chance at the mic. Tell him to move aside, because God's Word holds many promises and commands. And God says: do not fear, do not fret, do not worry.

FOR FURTHER REFLECTION

1. Think carefully about the ways you've been avoiding more Jesus in your life. What keeps you from joining a Bible study or from listening to sermons or podcasts? Are you too distracted by Instagram reels, TikToks, news, YouTube, Netflix, or your favorite sports team?

2. Now make a list of times that God has proven his faithfulness in the past: times he rescued you from harm, healed you, provided, sent someone to you at just the right time.

3. Whom or what do you most worry about?

4. Pray, right now, about those things. Then find a piece of paper, a note card, or a tablet and write that list. Stick it someplace where you will see it often, and when you see it, pray. Remind God that you trust his faithfulness and the way he will work these things out. Then, if you're still struggling, find a friend, share your list, and ask for prayers. Check in often to share how God is answering those prayers.

CHAPTER 4

Comparison Isn't Good for the Soul

The self-care ideology strives for a better life here. It searches for peace and rest and the ever-allusive happiness and continually offers another step we can try in order to hopefully attain those things now. At its core, there's something just ahead that should be better. If we breathe right, enjoy nature, or sit with a friend, something should shift. Fulfillment should happen.

To be clear, I love breathing. I work with people dying from congestive heart failure. When I had pneumonia during my fourth pregnancy, I often coughed until I gasped for air. It took a full year for my lungs to heal so I didn't lose my breath with minor exertion.

I absolutely love nature. Our family vacations revolve largely around experiencing the ocean, hiking to the top of a cliff, exploring a sand dune, trekking through a cave, looking at animals, or seeing whatever part of creation the area offers.

And Christian friends are the jewels in the Christian life.

All these things add value to life. But, ultimately, they point to the Giver. James reminds us that **"every good and perfect gift is from above, coming down from the Father of the heavenly lights, who does not change like shifting shadows"** (1:17).

Too often we don't realize how good things were until something changes. When our health fades, we think of how easy life was when we were healthy. When a relationship is strained, it's natural to look back to a time when things seemed better. When the bank account is empty or there's a person missing at the table, it's normal to wish things were different.

And while God loves to give us blessings to make this journey more enjoyable, our focus wasn't meant to be on the blessings or the lack thereof. The apostle Paul said:

> **I have learned to be content whatever the circumstances. I know what it is to be in need, and I know what it is to have plenty. I have learned the secret of being content in any and every situation, whether well fed or hungry, whether living in plenty or in want. I can do all this through him who gives me strength.** (Philippians 4:11-13)

Paul learned to fix his eyes on Jesus, not his circumstances. Circumstances will change. There will be years of plenty and years of little. There will be years of health and years of sickness. Our loved ones will die, and someday we will too.

God never intended that we become attached to this world or this life. Peter tells us to live as **"aliens and temporary residents in the world"** (1 Peter 2:11 EHV) because we're just passing through.

At creation, the plan may have been for us to live here in perfection forever, but from the second Adam and Eve chose to listen to Satan instead of God, plan B was initiated. And plan B was Jesus rescuing us by making the payment for our sin and death being the vehicle to take us to our eternal home in heaven.

Adam and Eve were cast out of the Garden of Eden, away from the tree of life. Death was a consequence of sin. Everything—all creation—became subject to decay.

It shouldn't surprise us then when our aging bodies struggle in ways they didn't before. And we shouldn't be caught off guard by death or disease. And yet so often we are, because the world encourages us to seek a better here and now and to find our heaven on earth. Satan and the army of evil tempt us to be shortsighted. He did the same to Jesus.

> **Again, the devil took [Jesus] to a very high mountain and showed him all the kingdoms of the world and their splendor. "All this I will give you," he said, "if you will bow down and worship**

me." Jesus said to him, "Away from me, Satan! For it is written: 'Worship the Lord your God, and serve him only.'" (Matthew 4:8-10)

Satan will gladly give you great gifts if they keep you from God. He will move you up the ladder so you get the prestigious job if it keeps you from church and God's people. He will gladly put friends and their love of motorcycles or snowmobiles or travel opportunities in your path to consume your thoughts and steal your time. He will nudge you to get the bigger house, the bigger yard, to have more, do more, want more if it keeps you out of the Word, away from prayer, and helps you fall in love with the world.

Satan will gladly give you great gifts.

The prophet Habakkuk gives a different view: **"Though the fig tree does not bud and there are no grapes on the vines, though the olive crop fails and the fields produce no food, though there are no sheep in the pen and no cattle in the stalls, yet I will rejoice in the** LORD**, I will be joyful in God my Savior. The Sovereign** LORD **is my strength; he makes my feet like the feet of a deer, he enables me to tread on the heights"** (3:17-19).

Habakkuk realized something most of us struggle to understand. If life is wonderful and blessings abundant but we don't have a relationship with God, we are in a horrific state. If, however, we have God on our side, no matter how dire our earthly situation, we are blessed.

We do not need more to be happy or even enough to be fulfilled. Enough is knowing Jesus and walking with him. Enough is knowing no matter how bleak life gets here, there's a home in heaven that already has each of our names on the mailbox.

That is why Paul said, **"I consider our present sufferings are not worth comparing to the glory that will be revealed in us"** (Romans 8:18). It's not about comparing where you are now to where you could be in a year or two or five. It's about comparing where you are now to where you will be for eternity.

That is not to say you can't have dreams and you shouldn't strive for anything. But your dreams and striving will include a closer walk with Jesus, being active in kingdom work, reaching more people with the gospel, and living like Jesus, who didn't let the pleasures of the world take him from his mission.

I've been working as a traveling nursing assistant for 14 months. When I first started, I had four or five money goals I put before the Lord. These were things that would be pretty hard to meet without that income. As the paychecks came in, I was able to make pretty significant strides toward those goals.

It didn't take long though for me to realize how easy it would be to make new money goals once those were met. I didn't want there to be a moving target of what I wanted. God, and God alone, is and would be my security, no matter what we had paid off or saved. It's easy to yearn for

more. We can always come up with new things to "need."
So while I spent 13 months working hard for money, as
those 13 months came to a close, I started asking for ministry. I began taking fewer shifts to make sure I had time to
do the kingdom work I'm passionate about doing.

Paul made tents for a season in order to fund his
ministry. We sometimes do just the opposite. We do
ministry for a season, but just a season, so we can get
back to making money and enjoying life.

What if instead of seeking pleasure and more we
pursued less of that and more of God? What would that
look like?

Day to day that may mean less phone and more Bible.
It may mean less work and more time to volunteer in the
community or with that organization that does amazing
outreach. It means fewer daydreams about things we can
buy and more days of getting rid of what keeps us from
doing kingdom work.

Every instrument needs tuning. When I worked with
a praise band, tuning the instruments to the piano was
the first thing to happen before any practice and always
before playing in front of a congregation.

Life in a sinful world easily makes us sharp or flat. We
chase after the things of the world or become dejected
for not having it all. Either way, we lose our focus on God
and the ministry he prepares for each of us. We forget our
purpose and wander from the plan.

We need to go back to God again and again to have our

hearts tuned to him. As we do that, God will use even the dark seasons—when we are sick or broke or persecuted—for good. Paul wrote letters to the early Christian churches when he was imprisoned. John Bunyan wrote *Pilgrim's Progress* from prison too. We can spend our days longing to get out of whatever isn't right or complaining we aren't somewhere else. Or we can ask to see the kingdom opportunities in front of us right now, even in the less-than-ideal days and seasons and places.

> We need to go back to God again and again.

We may have to get off social media to do this. During 2020 I limited my time on Facebook because mentally I couldn't handle the political discord. A year later I joined TikTok. It quickly consumed an hour in the morning and an hour at night and sometimes, oftentimes, more time in between. Influencers—people who make the best videos, who make us laugh and are healthy and beautiful—shape our thoughts and steer our minds.

After a year, I deleted TikTok. I want God to influence me. I want the Word to shape my thoughts and steer me to a different attitude and mindset. And if I compare myself to anyone, or strive to be like someone, I want it to be Jesus.

"'He himself bore our sins' in his body on the cross, so that we might die to sins and live for righteousness; 'by his wounds you have been healed'" (1 Peter 2:24).

Jesus left the glory of heaven to experience the discomfort of life on earth. He kept the commands that I continually break. He refused to go the route of pleasure and glory but sought only what his Father provided. He did not do what he wanted or thought best but what his Father willed. He was misunderstood and despised. He suffered ridicule, persecution, and death. For us.

He did more, gave up more, cared more. He resolutely stayed on task. He recognized Satan's schemes and refused to be distracted or coerced or coddled into anything that didn't align with God's will.

When I compare myself to Jesus, I fall short. My love has perimeters. His was limitless. I'm easily distracted. He had laser-sharp focus. He refused to be drawn into earthly glory and pleasures.

When I compare myself to Jesus, I'm reminded of his extreme love and sacrifice, and I too am motivated to live differently.

The writer of Hebrews said it beautifully: **"Let us run with perseverance the race marked out for us, fixing our eyes on Jesus, the pioneer and perfecter of faith. For the joy set before him he endured the cross, scorning its shame, and sat down at the right hand of the throne of God. Consider him who endured such opposition from sinners, so that you will not grow weary and lose heart"** (12:1-3).

Run *your* race. Don't worry about where you are or where someone else might be. Fix your eyes firmly on Jesus, who endured the cross and shame for the sake of future glory. Consider Jesus. He will give you strength and motivate you to keep going.

FOR FURTHER REFLECTION

1. Who and what influences you most?

2. What do you find appealing about that person, celebrity, news channel, or social media site?

3. How do those qualities compare or contrast with the life of Jesus?

4. What are your short-term and long-term goals/aspirations?

5. How can you fine-tune your goals to bear the greatest kingdom fruit? (Matthew 13:8,23; Mark 4:8,20; Luke 8:8,15)

CHAPTER 5

God Wasn't Messing Around With Rest

I tend to live with the pedal to the metal. I'm high energy and fairly productive. Until I'm not. I usually don't see it coming. Suddenly I stall, completely and totally exhausted.

As soon as I'm able, I get up and dive into the next project.

Here's the thing. Too many things burn hot and burn out. I've seen it. You've seen it. Ministries come and go. People come and go.

What is the key to surviving and even thriving for the long haul? Passion for sure, but rest is part of the soul-care equation too.

Our smartphones only go so long before they need to be plugged in. The car needs gas and every so often an oil change, new wiper blades, and a refill on the fluids.

In the Old Testament, God established a rhythm. He created the earth in six days. On the seventh day, he rested. God rested not because he was tired and creating took everything out of him. He rested because there was nothing more to be created and to set a precedent for his people.

When Moses gave the Israelites the law, which he received from God, he commanded, **"Six days do your work, but on the seventh day do not work, so that your ox and your donkey may rest, and so that the slave born in your household and the foreigner living among you may be refreshed"** (Exodus 23:12).

God didn't just give the law. He gave the reasoning behind the law. Give your animals and your workers a break. Don't work them to death. Let them rest and be refreshed.

He commanded the same for the land: **"For six years you are to sow your fields and harvest the crops, but during the seventh year let the land lie unplowed and unused. Then the poor among your people may get food from it, and the wild animals may eat what is left. Do the same with your vineyard and your olive grove"** (Exodus 23:10,11).

Again, the heart of God was full of compassion. His laws were not meant as a hammer but as a tool for watching out for the least of these. Let the poor gather what grows naturally, and let the wild animals eat what is there. Let the land renew its nutrients too.

This rhythm established a trust between God and his people. He would provide more than enough for them to store up in the other years so they wouldn't go hungry in the seventh year.

To work nonstop leads to physical exhaustion, but the spiritual consequences may be more dire. Especially if they point to a heart that refuses to trust God to provide and refuses to be content with enough.

For most of my adult life, I've been a serial offender when it comes to not giving my body enough rest. Working in a nursing home has cured me of that. The hour drive there, and especially back home, can be pretty daunting when I'm struggling with exhaustion. I've learned the harder I push my body, the harder it pushes back. My days become less productive. My decisions lead to declining health (sugar and caffeine to stay awake) and wasted time (because I'm too tired to do anything that requires brain function). I'm far better off allowing my body to recharge vs. pushing it to the limit.

> The life of Jesus is a beautiful example of how to live.

The life of Jesus is a beautiful example of how to live. If you want to know how to love, read the gospels. No one did it better than Jesus. Want to know how to stay on task? Read the gospels. Want to know how to avoid getting caught up in politics and all the rumors that come at us, how to resist the devil, or how to do the most for the kingdom of God? Read the gospels and study the life of Jesus.

When Jesus faced an exhaustive schedule, he made some important decisions. Mark tells us this:

> That evening after sunset the people brought to Jesus all the sick and demon-possessed. The whole town gathered at the door, and Jesus healed many who had various diseases. He also drove out many demons, but he would not let the demons speak because they knew who he was.
>
> Very early in the morning, while it was still dark, Jesus got up, left the house and went off to a solitary place, where he prayed. Simon and his companions went to look for him, and when they found him, they exclaimed: "Everyone is looking for you!"
>
> Jesus replied, "Let us go somewhere else—to the nearby villages—so I can preach there also. That is why I have come." So he traveled throughout Galilee, preaching in their synagogues and driving out demons. (Mark 1:32-39)

News spread throughout the town that Jesus healed a demon-possessed man at the synagogue. And then news spread that Jesus was at Peter's house. The people brought their sick, their diseased, their demon possessed to Jesus.

And what did Jesus do after all that work? He got up "very early in the morning, while it was still dark . . . and went off to a solitary place, where he prayed."

There's a meme that says, "There are two types of tired: one that requires rest, and the other that requires peace" (author unknown).

Jesus recognized his humanity required dependency on the Father. He sought and aligned himself with God's will as to what to do next. Then instead of going back to the crowds, he moved on.

The Savior of the world didn't have a savior complex. He wasn't worried that if he didn't heal those people, no one would. He knew God hears prayers. He knew God saw them and would provide, with or without his physical touch.

Too often our refusal to rest comes from carrying what we weren't meant to carry. If Jesus didn't feel a need to try to do it all, why do we? Do we really think our ministries, our families, our businesses will fall apart if we don't do everything? Few things hinge on one person. If they did, families, businesses, and certainly the church would have disappeared long ago.

If we are doing it all, or overdoing it at the expense of our health, time with family, or time with God, it's time for examination. Is your service keeping others from doing their part? Are they confident that you'll do it, so they put their time, energy, and resources elsewhere?

Could your need to control things be keeping them

from helping out? Are you open to new ideas and a different (not your) way of doing things? If Jesus was a control freak, he never would have sent the disciples out.

Too often it's pride that makes us think we should do it all or it can only be done our way. When passion is replaced by pride, we've lost our focus. We are on a road to burnout. And there's a good chance we've driven away the people who were more than happy to come alongside us.

The minute everything becomes about us, we're in serious danger of becoming ineffective. Our job is to serve, yes, but also to train the next generation to take our place.

On the night before Jesus died, he washed his disciples' feet and then explained:

> "Do you understand what I have done for you?" he asked them. "You call me 'Teacher' and 'Lord,' and rightly so, for that is what I am. Now that I, your Lord and Teacher, have washed your feet, you also should wash one another's feet. I have set you an example that you should do as I have done for you. Very truly I tell you, no servant is greater than his master, nor is a messenger greater than the one who sent him. Now that you know these things, you will be blessed if you do them." (John 13:12–17)

Until the moment he was taken captive, Jesus was

teaching his disciples how to live and do ministry without him. Doing it all has never been the plan. Serve selflessly, yes, but not to the point of not letting anyone else do the work.

There were times when Jesus tirelessly continued on, not because it was all about him but because he was compassionately caring for people. But we're also given an account when an exhausted Jesus was dead to the world.

In the first chapter of this book, I directed you to Mark chapter 4, recounting the sudden squall that came up while Jesus was asleep in a boat. Imagine sleeping during a vicious storm that threatened the lives of those experienced fishermen!

Jesus didn't let the craziness of life in a sinful world steal his sleep. Sure, he was all-powerful, but he didn't use his power to change world events. He didn't shift political dominance. He didn't provide abundant crops or correct religious mismanagement.

But he also didn't fret about those things. He saw everything. He understood, even more than the people, the evil behind Herod and other political leaders and the insidious nature of the religious leaders. If he was going to be up all night, it would be purposely spent in prayer, not in worry about the imbalance of good and evil.

How many nights have you been unable to sleep while you stewed over something completely out of your control? Jesus was resolutely concerned with spiritual things, and although he was always sympathetic and compassionate (feeding hungry people and healing those who suffered from disease and demon possession), he did not let the muck of life get under his skin and steal his sleep.

The prophet Elijah also came to a point of exhaustion, but unlike Jesus, it wasn't merely physical exhaustion. He had gone to battle with King Ahab and his wife, Jezebel, powerful leaders who led Israel into Baal worship. Elijah declared it would not rain on the land until he said it would.

Elijah wasn't cursing the land recklessly. He was trying to turn the hearts of the people back to God. Baal was the god of fertility. He was also the god of rain and dew, the two forms of moisture that are critical for fertile crops to grow.

If Baal was who Ahab, Jezebel, and the other worshipers claimed he was, surely he would send dew and rain. Surely he would see the people in need and come to their rescue.

But he didn't.

A three-year drought ensued. Instead of recognizing his sin and that Baal wasn't the god they thought he was, Ahab, no doubt influenced by Jezebel, blamed Elijah for the drought. He hunted him to kill him.

Finally, Elijah presented himself to Ahab and challenged him to a contest. Both would go to Mount Carmel. Both would prepare a sacrifice to their god. Both would call upon their deity. Whichever god responded was God.

The prophets of Baal did not fare well. Despite dancing and cutting themselves and crying for help, their sacrifice remained untouched. Elijah's sacrifice, on the other hand, which was doused in water, was completely burned up, altar and all.

Elijah commanded the onlookers to kill the prophets of Baal, and doing so put him at the top of Jezebel's most wanted list. Elijah fled for his life and ended up alone, discouraged, and overwhelmed under a broom bush.

"'I have had enough, LORD,' he said. 'Take my life; I am no better than my ancestors.' Then he lay down under the bush and fell asleep" (1 Kings 19:4,5).

No doubt Elijah hoped to wake up in heaven. Instead, he woke up to a heavenly visitor. An angel encouraged him to eat fresh bread baked over hot coals and drink water from the jar by his head.

Once he was refreshed, Elijah fell back asleep, only to be awoken a second time. The angel said, **"Get up and eat, for the journey is too much for you"** (verse 7).

God loves when his children come to him.

Elijah opposed the most powerful people in his corner of the earth, not because of their political ambition but because they led a nation into idolatry. He steadfastly followed God, even when he stood alone. And when he reached the end of his strength, God was there to comfort and renew him in a miraculous way.

When my body feels weak or my soul feels weary, I pray for strength. God is faithful to provide it. That doesn't mean we should balk at sleep and expect God to pull us through. But let's face it. Life is messy, and too often things happen in the wee hours. Other nights, despite all our efforts, sleep evades us. God loves when his children come to him in dependence, knowing and trusting that he is the source of renewal.

Jesus often withdrew in order to give the disciples rest. But rest wasn't always found. Sometimes the crowds followed (Mark 3:7-12,20), and when they did, Jesus didn't turn them away.

We will have seasons in life like that too. Small children need help 24/7. Sometimes aging parents or spouses do too. In those situations, when rest is hard to find, we get rest when we're able and pray for the strength to get through each day.

FOR FURTHER REFLECTION

1. Do you tend to push yourself to the limit? What boundaries have you set to make sure you don't burn out?

2. What situation or task have you been carrying that isn't yours to carry either at all or alone? How can you remedy the situation?

3. Some seasons are more tiring than others. If you're in a season when rest is hard to find, which little things might you need to give up in order to survive?

CHAPTER 6

Attitude Is Everything, and Gratitude Will Carry You

In the self-care world, Martha's sister, Mary, might have canceled Martha for speaking against her to Jesus. (I'll give you a second to mentally imagine Mary slipping her phone out of her pocket ever so discreetly to block her sister. Lots of good it would do as they lived in the same house, but that is neither here nor there.) One self-care list advised to unfollow the people who bring you down.

Thankfully, that's not God's way, or my list of friends would be small (because of me, not them). Paul's advice was just the opposite. He said to **"be kind and compassionate to one another, forgiving each other, just as in Christ God forgave you"** (Ephesians 4:32).

God's forgiveness is complete and without limit—total, forgiveness for every sin. God doesn't hold grudges or only forgive on Wednesdays before noon. Jesus shed his blood, and as he breathed his last, he said, "It is finished." Every sin we ever commit is paid in full. That's the way Paul tells us to forgive one another.

When Jesus came to Martha's house, Martha made two critical errors. The first was not keeping Jesus first. The second was being critical. A critical spirit is not a spiritual gift. In fact, it's just the opposite. A critical spirit will tear down and divide. We are to **"encourage one another and build each other up"** (1 Thessalonians 5:11).

Martha expected Mary to help, and when Mary failed to do so, Martha hit the roof. We play a dangerous game when we set our expectations and our attitudes according to the behavior of people, even those closest to us. It can seriously affect our faith walk or be a contributor to us losing faith altogether if the people of God don't act according to our expectations.

In Genesis chapter 6, Moses recorded: **"The Lord saw how great the wickedness of the human race had become on the earth, and that every inclination of the thoughts of the human heart was only evil all the time. The Lord regretted that he had made human beings on the earth, and his heart was deeply troubled"** (verses 5,6).

Every and *all* are convicting. *Every* inclination. *All* the time.

If you're old enough to read this book, you know that people let you down. Christians let you down. Your parents, sisters, brothers, children, spouse let you down. Your pastor or women's Bible study leader have let you down. If you know me, I guarantee I've let you down.

If we put our hope in people, we will be let down. If we put our hope in God, we will not. Unless of course, we are expecting him to be our genie. Even the disciples were disappointed in Jesus because they hoped he would be their political savior.

If we put our hope in people, we will be let down.

Once they understood the truth—that he was their spiritual Savior and an ever-present source of strength during this often-weary life on earth—their expectations changed. They rejoiced in suffering because it was proof that they were in the fight. God's people will always be at odds with this sin-sick world.

They came to understand that God never leaves or forsakes us, but that doesn't mean he gives us everything we want. And they understood that the pain and sadness of this life are fleeting in contrast to the glories of heaven.

Those truths are a fundamental shift in expectations, an important shift for us to understand if we're not going to fall into despair or turn away from God if he doesn't deliver according to our expectations.

As for expecting something from others: we can communicate our expectations, and we can teach and train. But we can't force behavior. Jesus didn't either.

The rich young man declined Jesus' invitation to follow him (Matthew 19:16-30). Many disciples turned away when

Jesus' teaching got hard (John 6:60-66). Peter denied knowing Jesus even after Jesus warned him that Satan was going to attack (Luke 22:31; Matthew 26:69-75). If these people turned away from Jesus and/or didn't listen and modify their behavior, chances are that we aren't going to fare much better.

If our attitudes are based on our expectations of people making the choices we want them to make, we will be disappointed. Instead, we learn to put our desires in the capable hands of God, remembering he doesn't answer prayer according to our whims. He answers them in the best way possible. And when we have entrusted our loved ones to God's care, we can go about our day with joyful hearts.

I know how difficult this can be. When one of my children decides to go their own way, it's hard not to let it affect my attitude. When the demands of the day exceed my ability to accomplish them, I easily become frazzled and frustrated.

Self-care ideology tells us to get it together and change the focus: "You let your bad days affect you too much. You don't let your good days affect you enough. Fix that."

The question then is *how*? What do I do to fix my attitude?

It *is* possible to maintain joy when things are falling apart. But I don't know how to do that without bringing God into the equation. When things get crazy, I turn to worship. The reformer Martin Luther said, "Come, let us sing a psalm and chase away the devil." I find that works pretty well, whether or not the song I'm singing is a psalm.

When my children were little, I often sang the "Create in Me." It's taken from Psalm 51:10-12. It says, **"Create in me a pure heart, O God, and renew a steadfast spirit within me. Do not cast me from your presence or take your Holy Spirit from me. Restore to me the joy of your salvation and grant me a willing spirit, to sustain me."**

Only God can replace my disgruntled spirit with joy. He can help me remember my identity on the basis of my salvation and citizenship in heaven. He miraculously and mercifully upholds me when things are falling apart.

For six months or so I worked the evening shift at a nursing home. For several months, one resident in particular was exceptionally difficult. When I changed his clothes to put him in bed, he would spit and kick and punch.

> Only God can replace my disgruntled spirit with joy.

It only took a couple nights for me to turn to worship. The go-to song in my head was an old hymn: "All praise to thee, my God, this night for all the blessings of the light. Keep me, oh, keep me, King of kings, beneath thine own almighty wings. Forgive me, Lord, for thy dear Son the ill that I this day have done, that with the world, myself, and thee I, ere, I sleep, at peace may be."[4]

It didn't change the resident's behavior, but it changed my attitude. I could concentrate on the blessings and ask for protection and forgiveness and peace.

After six months, I started working the day shift and was trained to give baths. I spent the day in a little room under a heat lamp running hot water in a tub, bathing the residents, and clipping their toenails.

It was the highlight of some of the residents' week. But there were others who hated baths. They were cold, didn't like to be messed with, grumbled, and no matter what I did, they complained that I was doing everything wrong. As soon as the water was running and was loud enough to muffle my song, I would sing the words to "Make Me a Servant," a song we taught the Sunday school kids at church. It speaks of being humble and caring for the weak.

Nothing about the situation would change, but God could keep my heart from becoming hard, resentful, and bitter. The focus was no longer about the people around me and how they were acting. I merely asked for a humble, serving heart no matter what I faced.

Worship is a powerful tool. So is gratitude.

Aesop said, "Gratitude turns what we have into enough." Most of us get this wrong. We think that when everything is as it should be, then we'll be grateful. In

---

[4] Thomas Ken, 1637–1711, "All Praise to Thee, My God, This Night," text public domain.

truth, joy is a byproduct of gratitude.

Remember Paul's words? **"I have learned to be content whatever the circumstances. I know what it is to be in need, and I know what it is to have plenty. I have learned the secret of being content in any and every situation, whether well fed or hungry, whether living in plenty or in want"** (Philippians 4:11,12).

Joy is a byproduct of gratitude.

The circumstances didn't touch Paul because he had already learned to be content. If there was food, he was grateful. If not, still grateful. If he was a free man, he'd use his life to go city to city telling people about Christ. If not, he'd talk to the guards about Christ and write letters and sing songs of praise to minister to other prisoners.

We too experience joy when we are thankful. If you're intentional, you'll find endless reasons to give thanks. There's the shelter you enjoy, the food in your cupboard, the family you love. If you have a church home and people who teach God's Word and forgiveness . . . if you know you have salvation and that you did nothing to attain it, you are blessed. If you can see past the pain to remember your home in heaven, you can endure. If you notice cheerful flowers and running water and feet that work and communication and garages and friends, you will realize how good you have it.

The more you look, the more you'll see. In his song "Falling in Love," Phil Wickham says that the more he praises God, the more he wants to. That's how it is with worship and gratitude. They produce the joy we long to have, regardless of the circumstances.

And they testify to others and Satan and God that we know God is still on the throne. When Job from the Bible lost everything, he fell down in worship: **"Naked I came from my mother's womb, and naked I will depart. The LORD gave and the LORD has taken away; may the name of the LORD be praised"** (Job 1:21).

Our storms don't catch God off guard. The book of Job shows us that nothing comes into our lives that doesn't first pass through the hands of God. Satan could only do what God permitted him to do, and God's watchful eye never left Job.

Our limited view and understanding means we rarely see the big picture. For that reason, we don't have to fret when chaos or craziness makes its way into our lives. Like Job, we can worship, declare God is good, and wait for God to deliver us to a different set of circumstances.

FOR FURTHER REFLECTION

1. Take an honest look at your life. Who are you expecting to act a certain way and suffering disappointment more often than not when they don't meet your expectations?

2. Make a list of hymns or songs or a playlist you can run to when you need strength to get through your day. Ask a fellow Christian for their suggestions too.

3. The most content people start their day by listing things for which they are grateful. Make a point to do so, either naming things out loud or writing in a gratitude journal. If there's a person who has helped you in the past few days or weeks, reach out to them and thank them for what they've done.

4. Don't just thank God for the big things. Thank God for the mundane, everyday things you take for granted: a warm cup of coffee on the deck, birds' songs, Christmas lights, your favorite pair of shoes, smooth roads, sidewalks, a winter coat, etc. List ten mundane things right now.

CHAPTER 7

Clutter Can Become a Hazard

Days before Hurricane Ian made landfall on Fort Myers, Florida, I sat watching the predictions, glued to the many videos on TikTok of Floridians packing and preparing. I was reminded that I have way too much. I wouldn't even know where to start if I had a few hours to pack everything I didn't want lost.

This is one place the self-care and soul-care worlds align. Several lists suggest decluttering your house, controlling your environment, taking 5 to 15 minutes every day to clean out one drawer or one shelf. (And that's how it took me an hour to make a cup of tea this morning. One shelf of spices and teas and condiments and birthday candles required sorting, throwing, cleaning, and organizing. The tea was cold when I drank it, and I'm not entirely sure I felt any more control over my environment, but I'm guessing when I make my tea tomorrow, it will be a more rewarding experience.)

Decluttering in the soul-care world has nothing to do with control. But excess easily becomes a hazard to our faith walks.

I was in my 40s before I learned this lesson. As I stare down the face of 50, I'm more resolute than ever. Stuff is a vacuum that—unless we're careful—sucks life, vigor, and energy that could be used for other things.

Marketers and advertisers have done a good job convincing us that more is better. Happiness can be bought if only we can get the latest, the biggest, the best, better.

> Excess easily becomes a hazard to our faith.

Here's the result: We work and work and work for more. The more we get, the more we have to work to keep it maintained and trimmed, painted, updated, dusted. Even seemingly "free" things take up space.

A hundred years ago people might have one picture taken during their lifetimes. Now our phones hold thousands of pictures. We transfer them to computers, buy more memory, burn them onto CDs. We have photo albums, scrapbooks, pictures on the wall, pictures on the shelves, pictures on our computers. So many pictures.

But when do we go back and look through the pictures? Who has time?

At the nursing home where I work, most residents have one to three pictures in their rooms. Typically, it's a spouse and their children, or if they never married, maybe their parents or a niece or nephew. And when those residents die and their families or friends come to collect their belongings, I doubt many of those pictures escape the landfill.

When my children were small and at home all the time, our house seemed so small. But as they've grown and now as they prepare to move out, our house seems ridiculously large. It's the people who fill a house who make it special, and when those people are gone, only stuff remains. At the end of the day, stuff isn't as fulfilling as one may think.

Stuff can't have a conversation. Stuff can't smile back. Stuff can't add meaning or value or health. It gathers dust. It can be swept away in a hurricane, burned in a fire, chewed by rodents.

Stuff steals the time we spend working for it, picking it out, maintaining it, throwing it out. If we aren't on our guard (and who other than a select few are), the clutter takes over our inboxes, our countertops, tabletops, entryways, closets, storage rooms, garages.

And all that stuff comes at a mental cost. An article called "The Negative Impact of Clutter on Mental Health" states, "Clutter can easily lead to a nearly constant feeling of frustration as you struggle to complete daily tasks. The time you spend looking for objects you need or attempting to organize your items could be time spent with loved ones, doing some self-care, or even just relaxing."[5]

---

[5] Kristen Fuller, MD, "The Negative Impact of Clutter on Mental Health, Verywell Mind (June 30, 2022), https://www.verywellmind.com/decluttering-our-house-to-cleanse-our-minds-5101511.

The mental health world recognizes clutter as a problem. In their eyes, it gets in the way of self-care. We don't always see the correlation between stuff and soul care. Who cares what my house looks like anyway? Who cares if I have more than one house or car or if I have a camper and a boat and a snowmobile?

Jesus. That's who.

He said, **"Do not store up for yourselves treasures on earth, where moths and vermin destroy, and where thieves break in and steal. But store up for yourselves treasures in heaven, where moths and vermin do not destroy, and where thieves do not break in and steal. For where your treasure is, there your heart will be also"** (Matthew 6:19-21).

This was my motivation when I downsized my possessions in 2020. I was tired of caring about and for stuff at the expense of having people in our home. Since our major cleanout, we've had people over often, held Bible studies, celebrated life, and mourned a death with friends and relatives. Years ago, that was inconceivable to me.

And once you get out of the whirlwind of the American dream, you aren't so quick to fall for it again. Do you really need another sweatshirt? Do you want that canoe or jet ski? Do you want the lake house or cabin or property in Florida?

Maybe you do, and maybe you will use it as a place to bring others for refreshment and edification in the Lord. I have friends who have cabins or a second home, and they've been a huge blessing to their families. They are a gathering spot and a place of refreshment. A couple of my friends even offer others a chance to stay in their cabin/second home when they aren't there. If that is the case, how wonderful for your family!

But we have to be careful with more. It easily becomes one more thing to clutter our minds, one more thing that requires our mental acuity, one more thing that has bills and keeps us from doing the things of God.

Jesus said, **"Martha, Martha . . . you are worried and upset about many things, but few things are needed—or indeed only one"** (Luke 10:41,42).

One thing is needed. One.

Jesus.

That's it.

Unbelievably simple.

Very few of us need a bigger house or more stuff. Rarely do we need another something. Maybe we don't need to work more hours. Fewer clothes mean fewer minutes trying things on. It means fewer things to wash. It means closets that have plenty of room. It means if you have to evacuate, a small suitcase and a few minutes would do the trick.

Can you imagine the limitations to the apostle Paul's ministry if he had a house full of stuff that tied him down? But very few of us are called to the ministry the apostle Paul had. So what does this mean for us?

Most of us in America have lived the majority of our

lives having plenty. But has that brought us more joy? Has that led to a closer walk with Jesus or to dedicating our lives to kingdom work?

Or has it kept us from more important things? Has it kept us from giving more money to missions and to believers on the other side of the world?

In my case, stuff kept me from hospitality. It is such a joy now to be able to share our home with others and not to squirm when the unexpected knock happens.

Don't misunderstand: things can be wonderful blessings. In my family, we have several snowmobiles because we live in the tundra, and it's an activity my family enjoys doing together. We have three canoes and a kayak too because we live in the land of ten thousand lakes and enjoy spending a summer afternoon on the river. We have way too many games that only come out a few times a year. But on holidays when extended family is giggling while strategically trying to outwit a cousin or grandma, I can't help but thank God for the afternoon together.

At the heart of it all is motive. If we're trying to acquire things for the sake of status or to help us feel better about our lives, we're bound to be disappointed. Stuff gets old, and it's hard to be on the edge of new and exciting.

Only God can fill us up and give us peace. Too many people seemingly have it all and are miserable. After all the weekends together at sports tournaments, the kids still leave home. After all the hours worked to give them more, they still walk away.

Stuff can be a blessing when we remember where it comes from and when we don't let it consume us. But we have to be careful about making a heaven on earth and finding security and happiness in what we have. It's all too easy to fill our lives so full of clutter that we have no time for kingdom work or guiding people to Christ. If that's the case, our stuff is just another tool Satan uses to keep us from our most important work.

FOR FURTHER REFLECTION

1. If you had three hours or less to pack up whatever you wanted to save from your house, what would you take?

2. If you had nothing holding you back, what ministry would you love to be involved in? Where would you volunteer? Would you spend more time with grandkids or at church? Would you start a new ministry/outreach altogether?

3. If you didn't have to work, what would you do with your time?

4. In light of all these answers, what changes would you love to make if it was possible?

5. Now take the first step to make those things possible. If not now, when?

CHAPTER 8

Zone Out Vs. Stop the Scroll

The self-care gurus face a dilemma. On the one hand, they suggest we find videos of fluffy animals to make us forget our troubles or watch a comedian to laugh again or indulge in a series or movie that makes us feel good. On the other hand, it's hard to avoid the statistics.

Reviews.org conducted a study around cell phone usage. The data shows that on average, Americans check their phones every four minutes. 47% of respondents consider themselves addicted to their phones. 35% admit to looking at their phones while driving. The average person spends nearly three hours a day on their phones.[6] That's not counting the time spent in front of a computer or TV.

---

[6] Trevor Wheelwright, "2022 Cell Phone Usage Statistics: How Obsessed Are We?" Reviews.org (January 24, 2022), https://www.reviews.org/mobile/cell-phone-addiction/.

In March of 2018, I was blogging for a women's ministry called Holy Hen House. This is what I wrote:

Too often I end up in front of a computer screen or TV screen or the screen on my phone. While waiting for my kids to come out of practice, I scroll. When the day has sucked my energy and I'm counting the minutes till I can shut my eyes, I scroll. At the dentist office, I scroll to avoid eye contact with other strangers in the room.

And after all that scrolling, I am still tired, worn, sapped, and empty.

What if we quit scrolling?

I decided to give it a try recently. Here's what I'm doing:

Instead of scrolling while waiting for one of my kids to come out of practice or work, I pray for that particular child. I pray for his or her health. I pray the Lord helps him/her to stand strong in the culture. I pray he or she walks with God all his/her days. I pray God molds and fashions that child into an instrument used to his glory.

At the end of the day instead of scrolling, I go to

my room and read. Not only do I get time with good books, but sometimes my husband and teenage children seek me out. In the quietness of zero screens, we talk and laugh.

After the kids get on the bus in the morning, I check my email, respond to messages, take a quick scroll down Facebook, and then I quit scrolling so I am ready for my date with God before heading to work.

In a short time, I've read through most of the second half of the New Testament. *(Truth in advertising: Philemon, James, Jude, and the rest of the books of the second half of the NT are quite short. It may sound like a lot, but in truth, it's doable for anyone who's willing to put in the smallest amount of effort.)* As I read, I underline what I think are the main points. I put a box around words that stick out. I pray. I am convicted and reminded I can do better. So and so is not the problem.

I am.

And when I stop scrolling, I notice how many people still are.

They scroll at red lights. They scroll while shopping with their daughter who is only ten once and asking if this dress is better than this one or should I use my birthday gift card for shorts? They scroll while the old lady in the waiting room who is alone all day watches, wishing someone would notice and talk to her.

While we scroll, time passes that we can't get back. Conversations that would have encouraged and blessed us don't happen. Relationships with our children and spouse deteriorate. Prayers we haven't murmured aren't answered. Spiritual growth that would have helped us navigate what is ahead hasn't happened.

And that's to say nothing of the 10, 15, 20 minutes we could have used to do the dishes, sweep the floor, talk to our neighbors, or sleep.

There's a better way. It's totally doable, and the payoff is substantial. Scroll less, and live more starting today.

I wish I could tell you that since 2018 that has never, ever been a temptation again. But that would be a lie.

In the past month, I've deleted an app I loved. I loved it so much it wasn't hard to spend two or more hours a day on it. I learned so much about nutrition and skin care from the videos I wanted to watch, but they were buried among so many other videos. I'd spend 20 minutes getting to the video I was hoping to catch. It's no different I suppose than the person addicted to lottery tickets. That one $5 or $50 or $100 win every so often is enough to keep them coming back to try again.

Time is precious. And it is so easy to waste.

As I've been working at the nursing home, I've noticed that other than being in the dining room for three meals, the residents have nothing required of them all day. Some spend their time in their recliners switching channels. Some spend hours in the dining room talking to the other residents, playing cards, and watching the weather. Some attend all the activities offered. Some take frequent naps. But few, very few, open their Bibles. Only a few read.

Time is precious.

I've always operated under the idea that after my children leave home, I'd have an abundance of time. Things that seem hard to do now would become easier.

I don't think that anymore.

We make time for what's important. If God's Word is a priority, we will open it. If we understand the spiritual battle we are in and the eternal consequences of not acting, we will engage in prayer and warfare for souls. Satan and the army of evil masterfully manipulate us all the time to keep us from making the Word and prayer a part of our day.

Remember Martha? She was distracted and almost

missed Jesus, who was in her house!

Throughout the Bible, we are warned and encouraged to avoid distractions.

- Proverbs 4:25: **"Let your eyes look straight ahead; fix your gaze directly before you."**
- Psalm 86:11: **"Teach me your way, Lord, that I may rely on your faithfulness; give me an undivided heart, that I may fear your name."**
- 1 Corinthians 15:58: **"Therefore, my dear brothers and sisters, stand firm. Let nothing move you. Always give yourselves fully to the work of the Lord, because you know that your labor in the Lord is not in vain."**

"Look straight ahead. Give me an undivided heart. Give yourself fully to the work of the Lord." (I just wrote these on a note card and taped it to the back of my phone).

The prophet Nehemiah mastered this. Nehemiah 6:1-4 says:

When word came to Sanballat, Tobiah, Geshem the Arab and the rest of our enemies that I had rebuilt the wall and not a gap was left in it— though up to that time I had not set the doors in the gates—Sanballat and Geshem sent me this message: "Come, let us meet together in one of the villages on the plain of Ono."

But they were scheming to harm me; so I sent messengers to them with this reply: "I am carrying on a great project and cannot go down. Why should the work stop while I leave it and go down to you?" Four times they sent me the same message, and each time I gave them the same answer.

You too are carrying on a great project. You might be raising children, supporting your spouse, being a hospitable neighbor, or carrying out ministry. You are a vessel that God eagerly desires to fill with his Word so that when you open your mouth, God's Word and encouragement come out.

This is our time to pray. We are the ones carrying on the work of the church or supporting those doing kingdom work. We can pray for those in ministry to make use of every opportunity, to resist the devil's schemes, to speak clearly about God and his Word. We can pray for open hearts to hear the Word, for Satan's plans to harm to be foiled. We can pray for marriages to be healed, children to be taught, that we are a light in a dark world. (I could fill the next three pages with ideas for prayer, but you get the idea.)

Phones can be such a useful tool. Time of Grace Ministry uses media to reach people right where they are. Through technology we can connect with people all over the world.

I love seeing what my friends and their families are doing. If it weren't for social media, I'd have to rely on the annual Christmas card to see what everyone is doing.

And the internet has blessed so many of us with information at our fingertips. I now have just one physical cookbook. If I want a new recipe, I look it up online. A few minutes later, assuming I have all the ingredients, I'm making it.

Family movie nights are some of our favorite memories. So much of parenting young adults happens when watching a drama or series and commenting on the good or bad choices of the actors.

But our TVs, computers, and phones can also steal precious time and opportunities. Unless we're deliberate, we can easily waste our opportunities to do important kingdom work or to spend quiet time feeding our souls with God's Word.

And rarely, if ever, has scrolling or sitting in front of the TV made me feel any better about anything in my life. If anything, it's just the opposite. I can't tell you how many times a series started out good but left me disgusted by the end.

It's not uncommon to feel deflated and defeated when I put down my phone. Once again, I'm reminded of the extent of corruption in the world. I'm left feeling less than someone else whose family has it more together or who looks better or can speak better or is doing abundantly more than I am doing.

I don't feel that way when I close the Bible. I don't feel defeated when I've given something to God in prayer. The pros vs. cons are not even close. Bible study and prayer are an easy win over TV, social media, and scrolling.

I'm guessing this is a struggle we all have. It's worth putting reminders in place: a Bible passage on the back of your phone, a book you've been meaning to read next to the couch where you watch TV. So much of life comes down to balance and prioritizing. If we're going to take soul care seriously, we have to at least be cognizant of how easy it is to waste time scrolling. Then, by God's grace and with his help, we can put parameters in place so that we use technology but aren't controlled by it.

FOR FURTHER REFLECTION

1. Sometimes it helps to schedule time in your day for certain things. If you were to schedule your screen time, how much time would you want to commit to phones and TV per day?

2. What books are on your reading list? How much time are you setting aside to read each day?

3. Contact your pastor or Bible study leaders for a list of books that shaped their spiritual lives. Visit your church library, and find a book that seems interesting. Then determine when you're going to read. Will it be

before work, on your lunch break, after supper? Will you retire early to bed to spend a half hour with a good book before turning out the light? (FYI: Studies show we sleep better when we turn screens off 30 to 60 minutes before sleep).[7]

4. Read the parable of the bags of gold in Matthew 25:14–30 for a refresher. God gifts each of us with talents and opportunities. If we are faithful, he'll give us more. If not, he'll give what we have to someone else.

---

[7] Matt Gratton, "Blue in the Face: The Effects of Blue Light on Sleep," Society of Behavioral Medicine, https://www.sbm.org/healthy-living/blue-in-the-face-the-effects-of-blue-light-on-sleep.

CHAPTER 9

Choose Friends Wisely

A popular quote says, "Show me your friends, and I'll show you your future." Motivational speaker Jim Rohn broke it down a little more. He said, "You are the average of the five people you spend the most time with."

Friends matter. They will either inspire and encourage you or tempt you, keep you from what's important, and lead you down a path of destruction.

Here again, the soul-care and self-care worlds align. The secular world recognizes the importance of being careful whom you let in. If all your friends grumble, there's a good chance you will too. If your friends smoke and drink excessively, you probably do too. If you are driven, you'll likely attract driven people. Unmotivated people tend to steer clear of ambitious people.

Now more than ever, we can hang out with the type of person we want to be. I've never met Time of Grace podcaster C.L. Whiteside in person, but I hang out with him often as I listen to his podcast. I follow a speech coach on Facebook. I love to listen to his videos for tips to use your voice to make an impact. Thirty years ago, that would have been impossible. Today we have access to all kinds of people with a click.

Therein lies the blessing and the curse. Choose wisely,

> Choose wisely, and you can learn and be inspired.

and you can learn and be inspired. Choose foolishly, and you'll have less time for God and the ways of the world will become commonplace.

Jesus said, **"A good man brings good things out of the good stored up in his heart, and an evil man brings evil things out of the evil stored up in his heart. For the mouth speaks what the heart is full of"** (Luke 6:45).

It matters what you put in. If the news anchors/commentators fill the news with fear and rhetoric, that's what comes out when you talk to other people. If you listen to the DJs who are hilarious but make raunchy jokes and normalize excessive drinking and/or drug use, chances are you'll repeat what they say or laugh about it with your friends who also listen. If you're soaking in the wisdom of a political commentator who trashes everything those in office do, my guess is you will be pretty upset and use every opportunity to mention how bad life is with "those people" in power.

The apostle Paul said, **"It is shameful to even mention what the disobedient do in secret"** (Ephesians

5:12). Shameful. Not celebrated, not condoned, not given the wink and smile. God's ways will either be archaic and insane or the path of life depending on whom you are around and who is doing the talking.

We don't have to listen just because it's on TV. We can turn the phone off. We can listen to a Christian podcast instead of a political one. We can read a biography of an amazing Christian instead of putting the trashy comedy on at the end of a long day.

If you've met your Christian friend group, it's easy to forget that twentysomethings who believe in God on a college campus are often the minority of minorities. We sometimes assume all children go to school in a building where they know and mingle with other believers. And if you haven't been in a nursing home lately, you'll find plenty of residents who don't want to hear about God.

It's easy to become the odd man out at any age and stage of life. When I started working at the nursing home, it didn't take long for me to realize I was in a secular environment. The language, the morals, the pervasive nihilism was eye-opening for someone who had spent most of her adult life volunteering at church and working in ministry.

Now, a year later, many of my coworkers, despite having very different worldviews, have become dear, dear friends.

Jesus was hated by religious leaders for eating with tax collectors and prostitutes. He ate with them and spent time with them and treated them with love. He didn't change his ways because of them, and he didn't condone the way they lived. In fact, when he was questioned for doing so, this was his response: **"It is not the healthy who need a doctor, but the sick. I have not come to call the righteous, but sinners"** (Mark 2:17).

When we become friends with the people of the world—whether it's a neighbor, a coworker, our in-laws, or the person who's always on the bus—choices have to be made. How will we respond when we're advised to embrace self-care, to zone out, to get something expensive for ourselves and concentrate on us because we deserve it and life is short? How do we meet the exhaustive comments about the economy, which we aren't dwelling on, because we trust God for daily bread?

God gave us his Word so we realize this is nothing new.

In the book of Genesis, we're given the account of Joseph, who was taken from his homeland to Egypt. By the time his brothers arrived 13 years later, Joseph looked Egyptian, sounded Egyptian, and fit in to the Egyptian culture. He didn't have a band of Hebrew brothers to hang around with. He looked the part but still knew and depended on God and was able to comfort his brothers with forgiveness and reassurance.

Daniel, Shadrach, Meshach, and Abednego stood out as Jews in the Babylonian government, and they were despised for it. Though they were wise and used their efforts for the good of the kingdom, their reverence for

God put them in a blazing furnace and in a lions' den.

Jeremiah was hated. Elijah was hunted. Elisha was surrounded by enemy forces. John the Baptist, some of the disciples, and the apostle Paul met their earthly end at the hands of those who vehemently determined to rid the earth of the name of Christ.

There may be plenty of times we're accepted and part of the group. There will be other times that our faith will not allow us to participate in the discussion. Always, our attitude and work ethic and language should testify that we are Christians.

Maybe they will think we're a little off. Maybe we're fine as long as we don't bring God into the conversation. But maybe when things go sideways, they will ask what we think, and in that moment, we may have opportunity to point to God who is on the throne above every situation.

What do you and I do if we find ourselves alone as Christians?

Early in my marriage, I found myself in that situation. Every time I became close friends with someone, they moved away. Each time was a differing degree of devastating.

Finally, I decided God would be my best friend. I dug into his Word. I listened to Christian music and Christian radio.

Through the years I've become "friends" with several people in ministry. Nancy DeMoss Wolgemuth, Alistair Begg, and other radio personalities have been my companions in the car or while making dinner.

Christian musicians like Tenth Avenue North and the David Crowder Band kept me company on many of my early ministry trips. These days it's usually Phil Wickham. None of these people know me by name, but they've ministered to me and been another person trusting God through the struggles of life.

You too can choose. Who are the voices you want to hear?

Who are the voices you want to hear?

As a Bible study leader, I'm biased. But in my opinion, the best way to make real flesh and blood Christian friends is to study the Bible together. Seventeen years ago, my husband and I joined an in-home Bible study. (That's not entirely true—I joined it and made him go. Though he wasn't super excited initially, it didn't take long till he was all in.) The people in that study quickly became our dearest friends. We shared life, prayed for one another, encouraged, supported, grieved, and celebrated together.

I've led Bible studies at two different churches in town and led online classes with participants from all over the country. Being in the Word bonds. Praying together bonds. Hearts open to the Word quickly become open to each other.

If you are a Christian feeling alone in the world, find or start a Bible study. (If you want a topical study and need materials, visit timeofgrace.org/store.) Typically, I study a book of the Bible. I use my trusted commentaries for background information and to make sure I know what the text says, and then I ask questions about how the text relates to life today.

A year ago, my husband and I started our own in-home Bible study. We handpicked a few friends, and for whatever reason, I chose to study the book of Judges. Judges recalls a time in Israelite history when they had already taken possession of the land of Canaan, but they didn't yet have a king. It was a time when wickedness ruled, and everyone decided what was right or wrong according to their own whims. The nation continually chose sin and idolatry over obedience and worshiping God.

We have been astounded at the lessons God has taught us as we've made our way through that book. I'm not sure why it's surprising to say that. God put the book of Judges in the Bible knowing we needed it.

I've just finished a seven-week series going through the book of Esther on my podcast, *Little Things*. There too God has reminded me of so many truths relevant to where I am right now.

You might be able to be a loner Christian, but that's not the way God intended us to do life. The Trinity, the very essence of God, is community. Father, Son, and Holy Spirit are in constant communion.

Esther had Mordecai. Daniel, Shadrach, Meshach, and Abednego endured together. The apostle Paul always had ministry companions.

If you're overwhelmed with life, struggling with fear, or overcome with anxiety, check the voices you're letting in and reconsider your five. If you are the average of the five people you spend the most time with, make sure they are the five who are going where you want to be.

FOR FURTHER REFLECTION

1. Answer honestly! Which channels, shows, or social media sites get your attention?

2. Which Christian voices do you turn to for direction? Why do you like to listen to them?

3. Who challenges you or holds you accountable?

4. Who most embodies the kind of person you want to be? How can you spend time with a person like that?

CHAPTER 10

Don't Let Church-Hurt Hurt Your Faith

I had no intention of including this topic in this book. But then I talked to the third person in two weeks who has left the church over the last several years mostly because of how they were treated by a pastor or called worker. If this doesn't affect the care of the soul, I don't know what does.

I went to the internet to find what the self-help world would suggest, not necessarily in terms of church-hurt but dealing with hurt in general. I found an article in *Psychology Today* that offered some good suggestions, albeit needing a few modifications to align it with Scripture. Dr. Gregory Jantz wrote "9 Ways to Respond When Someone Hurts You."[8] Here's a summary of what he said, along with my thoughts on it:

---

[8] Gregory L. Jantz, PhD, "9 Ways to Respond When Someone Hurts You," *Psychology Today* (February 2, 2016), https://www.psychologytoday.com/us/blog/hope-relationships/201602/9-ways-respond-when-someone-hurts-you.

One, investigate a little further. Was it a misunderstanding? Was it intentional or unintentional?

Honestly, how many arguments could end right there if we stopped to take stock of the situation? Unfortunately, Jantz suggested we listen to our hearts and follow our guts. We already know what God said about the human heart: it's only evil all the time. Better for us to investigate and pray, knowing God knows our motives and the motives of the other person.

Second, resist the temptation to defend your position. Simply let the other party know how you feel and give them a chance to respond, with the aim being mutual forgiveness.

I like that. One, you are going to the other party and letting them know what's bugging you instead of simply walking away without any communication; and two, the goal is forgiveness.

Three, give up the need to be right. After all, a disagreement means you disagree on something. That doesn't necessarily mean you are right and the other person is wrong. (I wish someone would have sent this piece of wisdom to me every week the first ten years of my marriage.)

Four, recognize and apologize for anything you did to contribute to the situation. Again, so wise. Very few situations in life are one-sided. Usually both sides contribute to the chaos. Jesus admonished us to take the plank out of our eye before worrying about the speck in someone else's eye (Matthew 7:3-5). By that he was asking us to do exactly what Jantz said and examine how we contribute to the chaos.

Five, respond instead of react. The idea here is not to just say the first thing that comes to mind (extraverts, take note!), but rather wait, take the perspective of the other person into consideration for a while; and then after mulling things over, determine the best response. Jesus' half brother James put it this way: **"Everyone should be quick to listen, slow to speak and slow to**

Maintain
an attitude
of love.

become angry, because human anger does not produce the righteousness that God desires" (James 1:19,20).

Six, concentrate on bridge building vs. attacking or retreating. Maintain an attitude of love whether or not you agree with the person.

That sounds like Jesus' words in Matthew 5:43-47:

"You have heard that it was said, 'Love your neighbor and hate your enemy.' But I tell you, love your enemies and pray for those who persecute you, that you may be children of your Father in heaven. He causes his sun to rise on the evil and the good, and sends rain on the righteous and the unrighteous. If you love those who love you, what reward will you get? Are not even the tax collectors doing that? And if you greet only your own people, what are you doing more than others? Do not even pagans do that?"

Seven, realize you may be the target of someone's anger but not the source of it. Oh my, if only I knew this five years ago. I would not have taken the attacks I endured personally. The familiar saying is, "Hurt people hurt people." That's not to say we excuse the other person's bad behavior or condone their actions, but it may change the way we pray and/or respond.

Eight, create personal limits. The article states that you alone have the right to set boundaries and insist they are followed. Of course, we don't want to let people continue hurting us. And there's nothing wrong with standing up for yourself and/or what is right.

But the world is quick to live by three strikes and you're out. More recently we endure cancel culture. If someone says the wrong thing or doesn't act according to your expectations, it's natural to cut them out of your life.

Jesus took a different approach. Peter wanted a boundary when he asked Jesus how many times he should forgive. Jesus responded with the parable of the unmerciful servant (Matthew 18:21-35).

His point: God forgives every thought and every word mumbled under our breath, every cruel thing we say, every horrid thing we've done. He asks us to forgive each other in the same way. When we finally understand the great many sins we commit and the debt we could never repay, it shouldn't be so difficult to forgive others. Equally important is realizing the point Jesus was making with the servant who owed much. We are depraved and fall into sin

all the time. When it seems unthinkable to forgive someone else for the way they've hurt us, we're often refusing
to see how our own sin offends God and hurts others.

And last, number nine: if someone hurts you, it need
not steal your happiness. The idea is that we can control
our emotions, choose to let go of the pain, and move on,
regardless of the other party.

The apostle Peter says this: **"Do not repay evil with
evil or insult with insult. On the contrary, repay evil with
blessing, because to this you were called"** (1 Peter 3:9).
He went on to say that God sees and responds. When we
are mistreated, it doesn't escape God. When we cry out to
him, he hears. Peter encourages us to continue to do what
is right and keep clear consciences, even if we suffer for it.

So what do we do when bad behavior by a called
worker hurts? We forgive, yes, but does that mean we
go back? The church is the one place we expect not to be
hurt, the one place we hope bad behavior is not accepted
or excused.

Is leaving church altogether the best option for your
soul? What do you do when there's not another Bible-
based church nearby or when other factors keep you from
venturing elsewhere?

The apostle John wrote his gospel after the other
three gospels were already written. That's significant
because if Matthew, Mark, and Luke had already written
about it, he either avoided telling the account again or
only filled in details the others didn't cover. As one of the

three included in Jesus' inner circle, he gave us insight into experiences others might not have known.

I have to wonder if he felt compelled to comfort those who had been hurt by religious leaders. Here's why I say that.

John recounted Jesus overturning the money tables early on in his letter (chapter 2). The People's Bible commentary explains, "From every indication, [the sellers] exploited the people. Greed gathered wealth."[9]

Where were the leaders to stop this from happening? In John chapter 3, we meet one, Nicodemus, who was intrigued by Jesus but too afraid to meet him during the day. Jesus challenged him and admonished him, but Nicodemus would not stand alone boldly until after Jesus' death.

In chapter 4 we meet the woman at the well. She was not anyone a civilized person would befriend. She was a perpetual screwup, falling into the hands of one man after the next. Her religious ideology was no better than her lifestyle. But Jesus showed his disciples, and us, that he came for her too.

Chapter 5 tells of Jesus healing a man who had been crippled for 38 years. Since Jesus told the man to pick up his mat, the Jewish leaders complained because it was unlawful by their rules to pick up a mat on the Sabbath Day.

In chapter 8 the Pharisees brought Jesus a woman (but not the man) who was caught in the act of adultery. They used her to try to trap Jesus. Instead, Jesus showed

---

[9] Gary P. Baumler, *John*, The People's Bible series (Milwaukee: Northwestern Publishing House, 1984), 44.

them their hypocrisy. He then told the woman he would not condemn her and she should leave her sin.

In chapter 9 the leaders had a fit because Jesus healed a man born blind.

By the end of the book of John, the leaders organized an unlawful meeting in a pop-up court in the dead of night, invoked the crowd against Jesus, and demanded his crucifixion.

All that is to say that the church leaders made it hard for people to come to Jesus, but Jesus wasn't bound by their laws, their prejudices, or their greed. He sought the needy and the broken and the lowly. He healed the hurt. People made their way to Jesus despite the leaders and despite the religious persecution they endured.

What does this have to do with those of us who may have walked away from a church, school, committee, or whatever else because of those in the church who hurt us?

Jesus didn't hurt you. They did. Jesus still wants a relationship with you.

The writer of the book of Hebrews encourages us not to give up meeting together. Why? So that we can spur one another on and encourage one another (Hebrews 10:23-25), in order that we might persevere.

To stop going to church because of the pastor or another leader is to miss all those people who are still in the trenches, all the people who would encourage us and pray for us and love us. It is like swearing off a restaurant because of bad service by one waiter.

In the last year, I've driven an hour to work four or even six days a week. I used to think that was unimaginable. Now that I've done it, it isn't so hard.

Why do we refuse to inconvenience ourselves, even a little, to meet with God's people, to join in corporate praise, and to hear God's Word? God promises his Word will do something. He said, **"As the rain and the snow come down from heaven, and do not return to it without watering the earth and making it bud and flourish, so that it yields seed for the sower and bread for the eater, so is my word that goes out from my mouth: It will not return to me empty, but will accomplish what I desire and achieve the purpose for which I sent it"** (Isaiah 55:10,11).

The readings and/or the sermon text will do something. They may give us hope, strengthen us, cheer us, or admonish us. If we listen with open hearts, the Word will work in some way in our lives.

Why then are we so quick to turn our backs on church when we've been hurt?

I'll tell you why. Because Satan knows there's strength in numbers. And he knows there's power in the Word of God. He knows prayers are answered and that the more people learn of God, the more they will love him. Satan's chief aim is to make us lose our faith and make us ineffective.

I would love to tell you I have no idea what church-hurt feels like. I wish I could say I am so far removed from it that I can't even recall the emotions. I can't.

But I can tell you without hesitation that God is faithful, and he will give you what you need to endure. I can positively assure you that Jesus loves the church, as messed up as it is. And the blessing comes when we remain faithful and refuse to let Satan pull us away.

In the first chapter, I told you about John Mark, his ministry failure and the disagreement between Paul and Barnabas. A lot of us want to end the story there. They each went their own way. God doesn't expect us to go back or work together.

But read on.

John Mark had a whole lot of important ministry work to do. And the apostle Paul eventually saw the man, whom he had considered a liability, as an asset, a ministry helper, and a friend.

God healed and reconciled. He put together what was broken.

He can do the same in your situation. Humbly seek him. Pray for restoration. Determine to find a biblically based church and go all in.

Our family didn't return to church for ten months after our church shut down during COVID. There was a time I wondered if we ever would. Church on the couch was pretty convenient. We could pause and make another cup of coffee and fast-forward through the hymns. We listened to several pastors, not just our own. Each week was like selecting a movie. "Do you want this service or this one? We watched that last week. Let's try this."

In all honesty, the thing that probably held me back most was the 15 pounds I had gained during those ten months. I distinctly remember thinking maybe I'd lose the weight and then go back. Again, good thing I didn't wait, because it didn't happen for another almost two years.

You and I need God now. If we wait till everything is as it should be, we will never go back. I have very few weeks when I'm feeling put together. But therein lies the beauty of church. We are all struggling and trying and leaning on God and each other. My going back made it that much easier for the next person who stayed home and cooked three meals every day and spent the evening on the couch in front of the TV streaming another episode of something.

And if you think you're somehow punishing the pastor or church leader by staying away, I would reconsider. Likely, you are losing more than they are. God tells us to let him be the one to settle the score.

There have been some struggles since I've returned to church, but they are miniscule in comparison to the fellowship we've enjoyed. Rarely a week passes when I'm not hugging someone or someone isn't coming up to me with open arms. I love catching a glimpse of my son talking with his coworker or his gearhead uncle. I rejoice every time I go to Lord's Supper with my parents or children. What a foretaste of heaven when we will enjoy the communion of all saints of all time!

Life is too hard to stay away from the fellowship of

believers. Take it from someone who knows. No matter how hard Satan convinces you to the contrary, the joy and love of going back are worth it.

FOR FURTHER REFLECTION

1. Make a list of the people who used to go to your church but haven't been there for a while. Have you reached out to them? If you're not comfortable doing that, commit to praying for them.

2. People in the nursing home miss church more than almost anything else. Sometimes one of the activities ladies will put an iPad in front of a resident and play a service. It is not uncommon to hear the resident singing along with the hymns and for others to stay nearby to hear too. If you haven't been in church for a while, what do you miss? If you go frequently, what would you miss if you were no longer able to go?

3. Of the nine steps to deal with people who hurt you, which two or three are the hardest for you?

4. Who is the last person who really hurt you? Have you taken steps to resolve the matter? If not, why not? Consider reaching out and trying to reconcile. If it doesn't work, at least you know you did your part.

Conclusion

As I finished this book, I just so happened[10] (please read that footnote) to be listening to a sermon by Alistair Begg called "Lost in Niceness." It was based on the account of the rich young man as found in Mark 10:17–31. By all worldly accounts, this young man was an ideal candidate not only as a Christian but to be a leader of the church. He had money, status, and he was morally good. But he couldn't part with his wealth to follow Jesus.

Begg said, "Any substitute god, whether it be wealth, materialism, relationships, whatever it might be, nothing, says Jesus, is allowed to come in between his follower and his kingly rule."[11]

This might be as shocking to us as it was to the rich young man, because one of the greatest struggles we're

---

[10] I say this tongue in cheek. In the Bible book of Ruth, we're told this: **"As it turned out, [Ruth] was working in a field belonging to Boaz"** (2:3). There's no coincidence in "as it turned out" nor in my "I just so happened." Clearly divine intervention was at work.

[11] Alistair Begg, "Lost in Niceness," Truth for Life (October 16, 2011), https://www.truthforlife.org/resources/sermon/lost-niceness/.

facing is our relentless obsession with us.

Does our comfort get in the way of following Jesus? Absolutely. Have you or I looked the other way instead of climbing in the trenches of other people's messy lives? I have. Does our pursuit of more interfere with our relentless pursuit of God? Yep.

I am 100% for the idea of taking care of our bodies. I struggle, but on my good days, nutrition is important, and so are rest and healthy boundaries. These things often come up in conversation and are on most of our radars.

Soul care, on the other hand, so easily gets pushed aside.

The rich young man walked away from Jesus because Jesus didn't offer what he wanted. He was more than willing to give his life to Jesus as long as it didn't mean giving up his comfort and his lifestyle.

We love lists that we can check off.

Watch the video. ✓

Take a walk. ✓

Breathe deeply. ✓

Call a friend. ✓

But a relationship with God is more than a to-do list. It's a lifestyle. It's seeking him in his Word, not as a chore but as a matter of watching intensely as he pulls back the curtain to give us a glimpse of him.

And while I love the idea of scheduling prayer time, in truth, I'm not so good at it. I'm better at having an ongoing conversation with God. As I remember things that are bigger than me, I pray, no matter where I am or what I'm doing.

And when I put down my phone and dive into books about God, like the one I'm reading right now (*Spurgeon on Prayer & Spiritual Warfare* by Charles Spurgeon), I am in awe of all I've missed and failed to comprehend. Those who give their lives to study God's Word know the Bible is many layers deep and a lifetime is too short to fully understand.

My soul needs to be fed the pure spiritual milk Peter talked about (1 Peter 2:2). It needs rest it can only find in its Creator. It needs exercise to make it strong to endure the trials and weariness of life. It needs the encouragement and fellowship of like-minded Christians to keep me from swerving off course or derailing altogether.

Soul care is worth our time and energy. The small investments we make—reading the Bible and listening to sermons and podcasts, reading books and commentaries, praying and worshiping alone and collectively—start changing us. Suddenly, almost without realizing it, we become passionately in love with God. Mundane things matter less. Getting our way isn't the object anymore. And we become bold.

The last day I worked before taking three weeks off to focus on ministry, I helped a resident in the nursing home to the bathroom. His body was filling with fluid. His heart didn't function well anymore, and he'd be meeting with hospice soon.

I wheeled him in front of the toilet and told him to rest a minute before standing, because even the simplest movements stole his breath. He admitted he didn't think he had long.

"Do you know Jesus?" I asked.

"I was confirmed," he answered.

I was so glad, only because it meant I didn't have to start at the beginning. (Parents, the time you invest in taking your children to church and teaching them the things of God is never a waste!)

In the next few minutes, I explained to this man that Jesus was the answer. That when we put our faith in Jesus, he forgives our sins and welcomes us into heaven. When you can't breathe, I told him, remember Jesus. Pray to Jesus.

Before I left work that day, I took a paper towel from the bathroom and wrote "Remember Jesus!" on it and put it on the table next to his bed.

He died soon after our conversation, even before meeting with hospice.

I don't know if he is in heaven, but my time at the nursing home has taught me I can't wait. Too often I don't get a second chance.

And I can assure you that there isn't a single thing I can think of—not a two-week trip to Europe or bonbons delivered to my house every day or a million dollars now and someone to clean and cook for me for life—that will come close to the elation I will feel when I get to heaven if that man is there.

Jesus asked, **"What good is it for someone to gain the whole world, yet forfeit their soul? Or what can anyone give in exchange for their soul?"** (Mark 8:36,37).

Nothing comes even remotely close to the care of your soul. The body dies, and all our efforts at taking care of it expire. But the soul lives on for eternity.

I want to see you in heaven. And I'm guessing you have a list of people you want in heaven too. The kingdom of God is in desperate need of spiritual warriors who battle in prayer and are bold with truth, those who see Satan and his lies for what they are.

> The soul lives on for eternity.

I don't believe in coincidence. If you've read this far, you know a lot is at stake. Put on your armor (Ephesians 6) and meet me on the battlefield.

About the Writer

Amber Albee Swenson has authored several books and is a regular blogger and podcaster for Time of Grace. Mostly she's amazed at God's goodness, awed by his wisdom and desire to grow her, and continually stretched by his calling in her life. For more details about her ministry, go to amberalbeeswenson.com. Listen to her podcast, *Little Things*, at timeofgrace.org or on Spotify, Apple Podcasts, YouTube, or wherever you get your favorite podcasts.

About Time of Grace

Time of Grace is an independent, donor-funded ministry that connects people to God's grace—his love, glory, and power—so they realize the temporary things of life don't satisfy. What brings satisfaction is knowing that because Jesus lived, died, and rose for all of us, we have access to the eternal God—right now and forever.

To discover more, please visit timeofgrace.org or call 800.661.3311.

Help share God's message of grace!

Every gift you give helps Time of Grace reach people around the world with the good news of Jesus. Your generosity and prayer support take the gospel of grace to others through our ministry outreach and help them experience a satisfied life as they see God all around them.

Give today at timeofgrace.org/give or by calling 800.661.3311.

Thank you!